GRAY MAN 2

INTERMEDIATE SKILLS AND TACTICS

Matthew Dermody

Gray Man 2: Intermediate Skills and Tactics
by Matthew Dermody

© 2021 Matthew Dermody

ISBN 13: 9798675229130

Printed in the United States of America

Front cover photo by Jana Sabeth via Unsplash

For additional book titles, please visit www.hiddensuccesstactical.com.

Other books by Matthew Dermody

Hidden Success: A Comprehensive Guide to Ghillie Suit Construction

Appear to Vanish: Stealth Concepts for Effective Camouflage and Concealment

Gray Man: Camouflage for Crowds, Cities, and Civil Crisis

Gray Woman: A Woman's Guide to Gray Man Tactics (e-book)

Hidden in Plain Sight: A Prepper's Guide to Hiding, Discovering, and Scavenging Diversion Safes and Caches

Conversational Camouflage: Oratory Discretion and Pretexting for Behavior Concealment

Situational Sense: Basic Threat Detection Using Situational Awareness and Common Sense

Going Gray: The Urban Concealment and Survival Anthology

A Not-So-Easy Target: Practical Tips for Protecting and Equipping Your Child

"Understand, it's time to get ready for the storm."
-    **Couldn't Stand the Weather, Stevie Ray Vaughan**

Disclaimer

Many of the techniques employed throughout this book are codified as illegal and criminal acts under Federal and State laws. Those same techniques are mentioned strictly for informational and entertainment purposes only. Any attempt by the reader to willfully engage or participate in the commission of criminal activity according to the law is the sole responsibility of the reader. Neither the author nor publisher assume any responsibility or culpability for the commission of any crime, or any injury occurred during the attempt of such acts.

Reviews

Table of Contents

Introduction 1

Chapter 1 – The OODA Loop Revisited and Red Teaming............. 6
See, Synch, Select, Start, Study, Scarlet Squad

Chapter 2 – The Shades of Gray 17
Sallow, Silver, Stone, Smoke, Slate, Soot, the Soviet Syllabus

Chapter 3 – The Psychology of Gray 31
Shades, Symbology, Stereotypes, Style, Speculations/ Suspicions

Chapter 4 – The Pros and Cons of Routine 42
Schedules, Sameness, Set-Up Scenarios

Chapter 5 – SAVVY – Wisdom and Common Sense 48
Specifics, Severity, Span, Stamina

Chapter 6 – Gray Man Communication 57
Signaling, Speech, Scaling, Sharing, Scouting

Chapter 7 – The Limitations to the Gray Man 74
Size, Scope, Surroundings, Situation

Chapter 8 – When Going Gray Does Not Work 89
Sensitization, Statutes, Sanctions, Stratocracy

Chapter 9 – The TROUBLE Kit 96

Chapter 10 – Stealth Supplies 114
Sidearms, Stealth Safes, Scanners, Sensors, Scrapping

Chapter 11 – Study Scenarios 124

Appendices 137

Glossary of Acronyms 145

Training References 150

Additional Resources 151

About the Author 155

Introduction

Except for my limited social media accounts, I have done little to promote and market most of my books. Having never been comfortable with mass-promotion or mass-marketing, I have relied extensively on word of mouth and the book reviews presented by other colleagues and survival enthusiasts. When I first wrote *Gray Man* in 2017, I did not expect some of the reactions it went on to receive.

In addition to all the positives accolades from colleagues and customer reviews, I have received my fair share of criticisms and attacks. It comes with the territory. One of the purposes of this book is to provide a constructive rebuttal to those who wanted more content; specifically, to include some "real-world" applications where adopting Gray Man principles provided a necessary, tactical, and life-saving outcome to a mission or other crisis scenario.

Despite the readers' desire for "real world" content, the very nature and purpose of the Gray Man does not bring practicing individuals into the spotlight for accolades and heroic recognition. Likewise, many of the situations warranting the use of Gray Man skills do not develop further, simply because the Gray Man skills deployed did not allow the criminal to execute their intent, resulting in a viable and reportable criminal act. If it never manifests to that extent, it neither becomes a crime statistic nor news report.

However, to address that criticism, many of the book chapters include a practical skill-set portion, including a dedicated scenario study chapter providing highly probable and hypothetical situations.

There were also requests for "practical" tips. As practical and practice share a common root, it is only logical to offer advice that is practicable, provided the reader is determined to do the work and make the effort to put the concepts into practice. A good percentage of what I am trying to convey throughout this work and my other books is an exercise in both self-control and personal behavior modification. As we can only change ourselves, our effectiveness in adapting Gray Man principles is deeply connected to how we self-manage our response to crisis and change. The bottom line: Adapt and Overcome.

For all the other criticisms, I must revisit *Gray Man*, review the concept of self-control, and follow my own advice. People are entitled to their opinions. Likewise, I do not have to justify, debate, or defend mine. To do so would be an exhaustive exercise in futility, as we have seen in the recent years that battling viewpoints result only in "agree to disagree" at best or to shame, name-call, and attack at worst. I am no different than everyone else regarding the entrenching of my position and not wanting to surrender. Besides, you never surrender when you are winning or on the side of right.

Some critics are so heavily indoctrinated in the politically correct culture that they cannot look objectively beyond their own cognitive and confirmation bias while reprimanding me for mine. Their behavior only points out the fact which I explained in the book that every human on the planet has and uses bias. I had clearly stated that it was not my intention to disparage or malevolently engage in any type of discrimination, only acknowledge its presence. There is no other oppressive or hate-motivated reason behind the discussion of stereotypes in any of my books. However, I will provide a statement to the handful of people who chose to accuse me in reviews. I strongly object and denounce those accusations levied against me. That is all I am prepared and obligated to say on the matter.

The elements within society which prompt individuals to adopt and implement Gray Man tactics are controversial, indeed. Events such as riots, civil unrest, governmental overreach, and potential exposure to criminal behavior all warrant its justification. Those who utilize Gray Man skills do so because they recognize the need to adjust their behavior to be vigilant and on guard against deviant members of society. When others engage in behavior that is either codified as criminal or not acceptable to other members of society, we need to prepare accordingly to condemn and, if necessary, confront that behavior. To paraphrase the late Jeff Cooper, criminals do not fear laws, the police, or the court system; so, they must be made to fear their potential victims and the rest of the citizenry who must be willing and ready to stand up against them.

We are seeing this unfold right before our eyes. Riots and looting are emerging in largely urban and downtown areas. City centers are under siege, services are crippled or reduced, and city officials are cowardly surrendering taxpayer funded sites and services to angry mobs of people who choose to behave like toddlers throwing tantrums because they did not get what they wanted. Regardless of the real or imagined slights against them, there is a proper and lawful way to address grievances and it is clear those options are being dismissed for the sensationalism of direct violence and chaos.

This book is closer to a third installment rather than a sequel. Having introduced the concept of Situational Sense in *Gray Man* and seeing an opportunity to expound upon the subject, I wrote *Situational Sense*, knowing it would fit in with the overarching concepts presented in *Gray Man*. It is important to note that the two are not one in the same. You can be situationally aware, but not a gray man. However, you cannot be a gray man, without being situationally aware.

There have also been books written by others who have made statements with whom I do not share the same opinion. This does not necessarily disqualify their overall knowledge of the subject, nor does it mean that everything they say should be taken as Gray Man gospel. I am quite certain others feel the same way with some of the things I have addressed in earlier books. However, a few of these statements must be pointed out and clarified.

One statement was that a Gray Man is someone who "effortlessly" blends into his surroundings. Obviously, I take issue with the word *effortlessly* because *it does take* a conscious, ever-watching and ever-evolving effort to blend into an environment where maximum concealment efficiency is desired and ultimately gained.   Another comment asserted, "By the end of this book, *you will learn everything you need to know* about why and when you need to become a gray man and how to be one." Despite being recognized as a subject matter expert in certain professional communities, I have never made such an arrogant statement. Anyone familiar with the concept of the Johari window for self-awareness, will see the error of claiming to know everything about a subject. It is riddled with cognitive bias.

The final reason is, like many others trying to learn about the Gray Man subject, I too, am still learning. It is a never-ending cycle. I am not the be-all/end-all expert regarding the Gray Man subject, nor have I ever stated as such.   I continue to do as I promised in my earlier books...what I learn, I pass on. As society and technology evolve to improve detection methods, we must continue to invent and develop ways to counteract those attempts and thwart their intentions.   The goal is, hopefully, to become proficient enough where we do not or cannot recognize or identify our fellow practitioners all the time. That, too, will be a learning and adaptation curve that will not cease.

John Boyd's OODA Loop has long been a staple of every situational awareness and Gray Man curriculum I have seen or heard about. It is taught everywhere from corporations to firearm training centers to local self-defense schools. As you may remember, OODA is an acronym for Observe, Orient, Decide, Act.

While I typically believe the "if it ain't broke, don't fix it" mantra, I see nothing wrong with customizing things a bit for the sake of some originality. To adapt Boyd's work into the teaching framework I use and make it uniquely presentable, I have modified it to blend into the ongoing S-word alliteration I began years ago. While the words change, the human behaviors occurring in response to the new words used are very much the same. I call it a Sense Sphere. This is by no means meant to detract from the original name, but it does expand upon some important elements to consider within each phase of the loop. The next section will help explain the reasoning behind those key elements.

The Sense Sphere

The sphere is a geometric shape that is three-dimensional. As such, everything in our world has a relationship with the specific dimensions of height, width, and depth. When viewed from this three-dimensional perspective, we can see as it rotates, there is another angle to view which may shed additional light or provide another vital piece of information to aid in the execution of a step or to proceed to the next. When viewed in only a two-dimensional paper model, it loses some perspective. If a three-dimensional sphere is added to the illustration, it provides that strong inference to view all situations from every plausible and relevant viewpoint. Obviously, there are times that demand a faster response and less time spent on any one phase. But that should not limit or deter one from looking at as many different angles and possibilities as time and circumstances will allow.

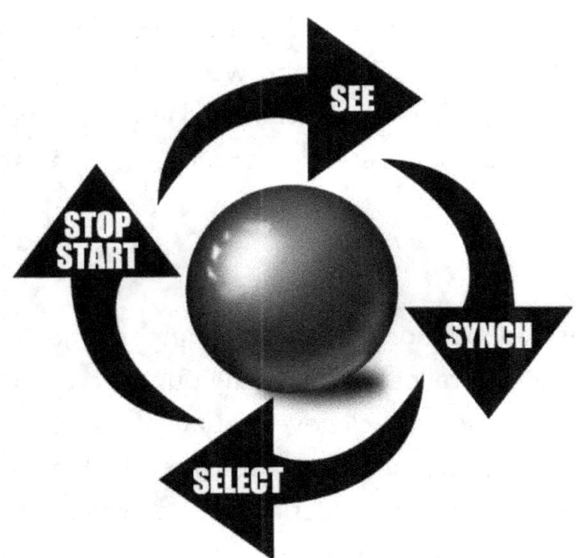

The Sense Sphere, the author's interpretation of Boyd's OODA Loop. Graphic by author.

SEE - Observe
SYNCH - Orient
SELECT - Decide
START/STOP - Act

As I mentioned, it is not to detract from the original Boyd model. However, for me, the renaming to *See*, *Synch*, *Select*, and *Start* seems to flow faster and contains fewer syllables. Maybe this works better for you or maybe it does not.

SEE (Scan, See, and Study the surroundings)

Scan/See

Just like many people in the world, I am a visual learner. I learn best from watching and observing. After I have watched something performed enough times, I move into the second learning level of doing. A great deal of the contextual meaning we perceive is gathered through our sensory organs, with most of it collected visually. Therefore, seeing is the primary method of observation and information gathering.

Study

Study is a foundational behavior to understand and process the ever-changing circumstances surrounding our everyday lives. I always mention study because you will never get away from it, nor should you want to stop studying. It is an observation method that joins forces with your previous knowledge and experiences. You can bet that any book I write, you will find a clear admonishment to study. When you are not studying, you should be practicing.

Studying and applying scholarly concepts to the art of learning will give you a broader base of knowledge on related subjects to develop and give credence to:

- Identifying and exploiting assets
- Creating pretexts and alibis
- Forming legitimate justifications
- Developing solutions to problems

SYNCH (Synchronize and Stabilize to the surroundings)

Stabilization and synchronization sometimes occur simultaneously in response to our minds rapidly processing the incoming data from the environmental stimuli collected in the study phase. We quickly adapt and adopt societal cues and expectations to ensure we do not bring unwanted or unnecessary attention to ourselves, violate some unspoken protocol, or avoid certain types of conflict.

So, as we are studying the environment in which we find ourselves, we stabilize and synchronize our actions and mannerisms to conform with the established baseline within the culture or society. We must adjust...sometimes to the detriment of our personal comfort or beliefs. However, that synching with environmental baseline now provides for some level of anonymity to move around unnoticed.

SELECT (Scrutinize and Select the course of action)

The earlier we can detect potential danger ahead; it gives us more options to consider and act upon. However, the longer we stay oblivious to those early warning signs, our options reduce significantly to the point where we may only have a single choice. This is obviously not how we want to meet dangerous situations, where the remaining choice or choices require an over-reliance on outside help or the sacrifice of something of value.

START (Start or Stop the necessary course of action)

The major difference to Boyd's call to action in his model compared to mine is my addition of the word stop. Sometimes the required action is not necessarily to start doing something, but rather stop doing something or stop someone else from committing a particular action.

The will to act is deeply rooted in mindset. It takes a warrior's mindset. Our decision to physically act and get into motion or sit and suffer are linked to the mindsets we develop prior to problems developing.

One of the more profound examples I found describing how we orient in a particular environment and adjust our situational sense/awareness skills is in the classic 1973 martial arts film, *Enter the Dragon*, starring the late Bruce Lee. The climatic final battle with the drug lord Han provides an interesting take on one's ability and need to rapidly adapt to the environment.

In the final showdown, Han has retreated into mirrored room accessed by a revolving panel door. Bruce Lee follows Han into the room and is immediately disoriented by the countless reflections of himself. His unfamiliarity with the room itself, puts Bruce at a severe disadvantage. As a result, Han armed with a triple-bladed prosthesis, was able to utilize sneak attacks against Bruce.

As a teen watching this, I never understood why Bruce began kicking and breaking all the mirrors. (Later cuts of the film added the voice-over of Bruce's master explaining that an enemy uses imagery and illusion, alluding that one must destroy the image to defeat the enemy.) I had initially thought he was blindly kicking at every appearance of Han in the hopes of finding the real version of the villain. Later, I realized that with every mirror cracked, the only version of Han able to get close enough to strike would be the real Han, as he would not appear broken and shattered. With all the mirrors intact, Han could move freely in his illusion room, but with the mirrors shattered, he no longer had the advantage of duality and multiple projections to aid him. As a result of Bruce's ability to adapt and orient to the environment, he was able to defeat Han.

Scarlet Squad

Another important thing to consider within with the OODA Loop/Sense Sphere is the concept of the Scarlet Squad. Scarlet Squad is nothing more than the continuance of my "S- word" alliteration teaching method, which in this case, directly references Red Teaming. Red Teaming is a highly detailed, comprehensive simulation strategy and evaluation protocol utilized to analyze how well a company or organization (its people, networks, applications, and security controls) respond to and withstand real-life adversarial attacks.[1]

The military often uses this type of assessment to test the vulnerability of military units. One of the ones I am most familiar with is the utilization of the Navy SEALs to test fleet vessels. It had two main advantages as it provided the necessary evaluation of combat readiness and vulnerabilities of a ship and its crew, while providing the SEAL Teams an effective and realistic training scenario for boarding and commandeering nautical vessels. The SEALs were (and still are) famous for never willfully accepting failure, while the ship's commanding officers were adamant about the consequences that would result from being "embarrassed" should the SEALs be successful. The embarrassment was more common among the ship's company than SEAL team failure during these exercises.

One of the interesting aspects of red teaming I found while researching the subject is the simple, four element approach to strategizing and planning. The four elements consist of: Observe the Patterns, Make a Plan, Blend in, and Execute.[2] This is straightforward and manageable, without getting too caught up in unnecessary tangents or irrelevant information.

To go along further with plan development, there is an acronym frequently used towards the conceptualization of multiple plans called PACE.[2] Each letter in the word PACE stands for an individual plan to accomplish a singular objective. Therefore, I add the letter "S" to make SPACE, as a reminder for the singularity in purpose, in objective, and in outcome. It becomes the bottom line, one-thing that must be accomplished. It means keeping the main thing the main thing. Plans that attempt to multi-task set themselves up for failure and risk becoming convoluted and murky when one or more of the proposed objectives go sideways due to interference often interjected by Mr. Murphy.

S – Singularity

P – Primary

A – Alternative or Alternate

C – Contingency

E – Emergency or Escape

By implementing the concept of red teaming, you are preparing for and have protocols in place to make your Gray Man efforts more successful. Thinking like your enemy allows you to do a couple of things. First, it should make you respect the potential of an adversary. Your enemy may be just as motivated, dedicated, and trained to subject you to the very thing you wish to resist or prevent. Second, it will inspire a level of confidence that your plan will have the highest chances for success knowing you have considered many, or possibly all, of the enemies counter moves. Third, a level of preparedness through supplies, training, and scenario rehearsals will also reinforce and bolster that confidence throughout all the planning stages.

PRACTICAL SKILL-SET:

Choose a regular activity and then plan and develop four sets of actionable steps and responses to complete that activity in accordance with the described PACE method. This is only to familiarize yourself with formulating multiple plans which can then expand into larger, more complex activities as needed.

Activity: ____

Primary:

____

____

____

____

____

Alternate:

____

____

____

____

____

Contingency:

____

____

____

____

____

Emergency:

____

____

____

____

Execute each plan and then objectively review them, specifically looking for steps and procedures to improve, eliminate, or replace, as necessary.

If you would like to apply this strategic planning method to other activities, simply copy the format down in your own emergency action plan (EAP) folder.

Another format available to develop your own exit contingency plan is the **L.E.A.V.E.** model:

L – **LOCATE** exit points.
E – **EVADE** hostile threats.
A – **ACCESS/ACTUATE** mechanisms/locks to facilitate exit.
V – Maintain **VIGILANCE**.
E – **EXIT** to safety.

This model can be used in new or unfamiliar areas where there may not have been sufficient time for prior scouting and reconnaissance or when an emergency evacuation is necessary.

Sources and citations:

[1]https://redteams.net/the-4-elements

[2]https://www.redteamsecure.com/blog/what-is-red-teaming-and-why-do-i-need-it-2/

I feel many people prefer and seek a world of absolutes. They desire clear, definitive lines between right and wrong, good and evil, order and chaos, justice and lawlessness, peace and war. I also believe the majority of humanity wants what is right, good, orderly, just, and peaceful. The heartbreaking reality is there are those who willfully, wantonly do not want those things. Those who do not want peace willfully choose violence to coerce, manipulate, and intimidate others. Violence offered as a defensive response is vastly different from a moral viewpoint, but still considered a last resort.

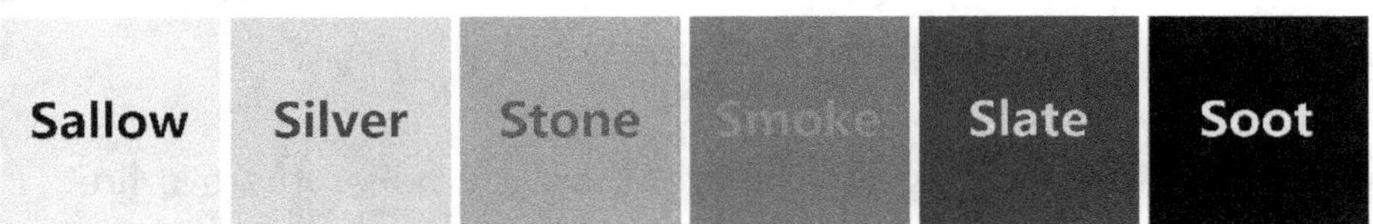

The Gray Man color code. Illustration by author.

You must determine what shade of gray you are willing and comfortable operating and living in. Admittedly, my admiration of Colonel Jeff Cooper's combat mindset (often referred to as Cooper's Color Code) provides the basis and inspiration for the Gray Color Code previously shown. Living in the Sallow category is unacceptable for any Gray Man practitioner. Most people will find existing within the middle three gradients the easiest and most practical. Going beyond that into the realms of Slate and Soot are almost the equivalent of "going dark" and "going black" in field operative speak.

Sallow – While not a common word, its meaning is well known by its other common names: pale and sickly, or ashen. The expression "pale as death" comes to mind; and if you are not paying attention to what is happening around you, what you are doing, and where you are going, the greater your chance of becoming a victim and statistic.

Silver – Just as the name implies, the silver zone is a bit flashier. You can get away with wearing jewelry, a fancier watch, or trendier clothing and it would not make you stand out any more than the average person. I would not recommend this from a personal safety standpoint or if in unfamiliar territory, but if you are paying attention to your surroundings, you could wear a fancier watch or conservative jewelry.

Stone – This zone implies a hardening up to make yourself less of a target. I liken it to having a poker face, where the objective is to mask any facial expression regarding the hand one is holding, or in this instance, the knowledge and skills one holds.

Smoke – The old saying "Where there's smoke, there's fire" is appropriate in this zone. There is a specific, definitive threat near or around you and you need to use the confusion and chaos to mask your movements. Just like in a fire, smoke escapes through any opening it can find. Once in the open, it has the potential to quickly dissipate and disappear based on conditions.

Slate – The Slate zone is hard like granite and can be very dark. I am reminded of the expression, "a clean slate" and is almost to the point of starting over. This would be considered extreme for the purposes of this book and there are already books written on the subject of disappearing if one had the interest or prerogative to study it further.

Soot – The Soot zone would represent the blackened fallout from a complete societal collapse where the only course of action is to start over. Unlike the Slate Condition, which operates under the premise of being voluntary, the Soot Condition almost dictates the need to reset.

The two extremes, sallow and soot, would obviously want to be avoided, and so we find ourselves dwelling within the realms of the inner four conditions, giving us the freedom to move and flow as situations dictate.

The Enemies of the Gray Man

Enemy is a powerfully provocative word, especially when trying not to create excess stimuli in those who observe us. Because the color gray is often portrayed as devoid of a clear delineation of good and evil, or possessing both good and evil characteristics, there are those who will view us as a threat or an adversary at some point, regardless of our efforts to minimize undesirable stimuli.

You may recall the circle of trust illustration from my other books or from social media posts. In essence, all the active and passive provocateurs listed below dwell within the outer ring of society described as the savages; those who may directly or indirectly try to shorten your existence. Simply put, anyone who is not actively or passively helping you is a potential threat.

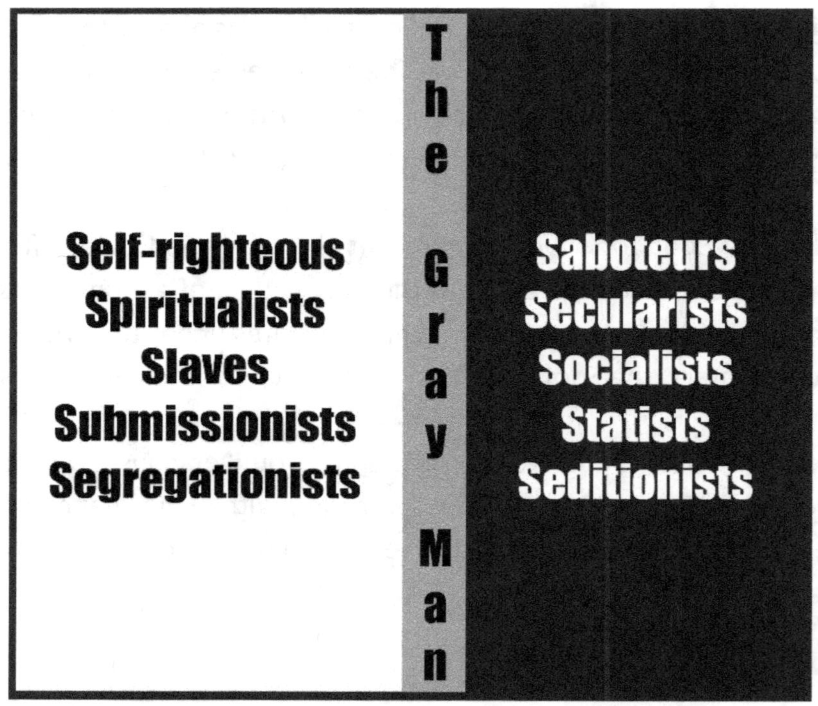

The enemies of the Gray Man. Illustration by author.

To further complicate this concept of "enemies", the term is not indicative of people, but rather the ideologies which drive them to engage in behaviors that do not have you in their best interest. As such, their philosophies and ideologies are the issue rather than the individual themselves. That does not mean the individual is not a threat, but you are not looking at the person as the root cause or solely responsible for the belief system motivating them into action against you.

There used to be an expression, that when first spoken, was likely meant as a bit of a comedic quip, "It's not paranoia if they really are after you." Unfortunately, the saying is becoming a reality in today's polarized political and social climates. It is apparent in the narratives on the nightly news and the speeches made by politicians. Make no mistake, the ideologies of the savages are here and are merely waiting for the word to come after your possessions.

Indirect Savages

The *self-righteous* refuse to help as they believe you have brought the circumstance upon yourself through your own choices and actions. Nor do they wish to be affected by the same consequences, so they refuse to offer association or assistance.

The *spiritualists* offer no solace beyond the outcome being in the hands of deity or destiny, claiming any participation on their part will violate the divine will of God and His judgement. Some will chalk it up to karma or fate.

The *slaves* do not want you to rock the boat and put what little comforts they have at risk. They will dissuade you, even up to the point of violence to keep themselves under the radar.

The *submissionists* simply roll over, refusing to fight and accept whatever reward or reproach is offered to them. These people are cowards and unfortunately, there is not a nicer way to say it.

The *segregationists* have chosen to isolate themselves from the rest of the world and care only for their own. If you do not fit in or align with their ideology, they have little interest in offering support.

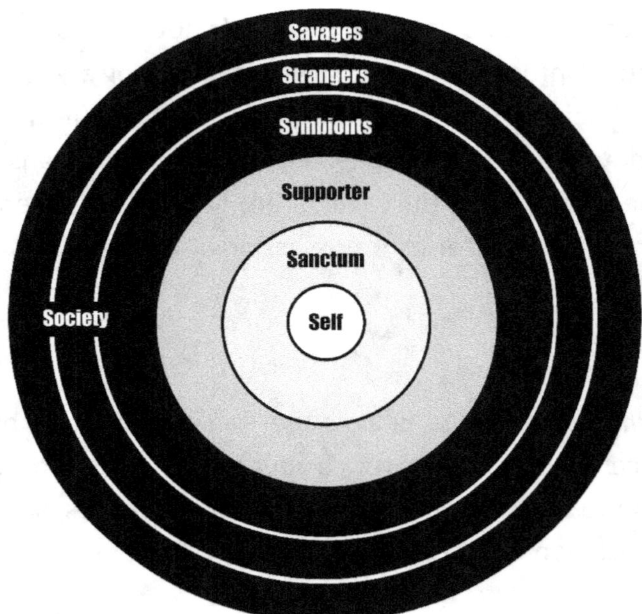

The Circle of Trust. Illustration by author from the book *Conversational Camouflage*.

Direct Savages

The *saboteurs* want only to hinder or prevent you from enjoying what little freedoms you have left. They will destroy your efforts and aid those want to reduce your freedom, your productivity, and your resistance to an agenda of dominance through oppression.

The *secularists* want to destroy the last bastions of hope and faith, making you look to your fellow man as your only source for all things.

The *socialists* want to take everything you have earned through coercion and force to divide it amongst those cannot or refuse to work themselves.

The *statists* want nothing in your control, surrendering everything to government oversight and regulation, reducing rights to privileges. They will pile law upon law, regulation upon regulation, where you can no longer financially afford your "rights" or you become labeled as a criminal under unjust laws, should you choose to fight to keep those rights.

The *seditionists* want to overthrow the republic and install a new hostile form of government, removing the concept of self-rule of the people. Oddly enough, sedition is also being thrown around to describe people resistant to the governmental changes that are clearly on the horizon.

When these people start showing up on your doorstep or begin confronting you on the street, you will have terrible choices to consider. None of the choices are pleasant and none of the choices should have to be made if we had adhered to the type of government and rule of law envisioned and started by our Founding Fathers.

This is a good point to reference back to some Situational Awareness ABC's for when these types of scenarios manifest.

A- Alert
B- Brave
C- Careful
D- Decisive
E- Explosive
F- Ferocious

You should always be mindful of the first three: Alert, Brave, and Careful; and willing to be Decisive, Explosive, and Ferocious if needed.

As soon as I mentioned socialists in the Direct Savages section, my thoughts immediately gravitated to the former Soviet Union. During the height of the Cold War growing up in the 70s and 80s, the talk of communism and the Soviet Union were often the subject of the nightly news and the subject of nearly every action-adventure movie released during that time period. The Soviets were always portrayed as the bad guys and America was heroically poised to prevent the spread of communism into the rest of the free world.

It is important to remember, despite what is depicted in movies and TV show, the Russians then, like many of our national enemies now, are not and were not bumbling idiots or mindless cannon fodder who do not possess tactical or technical knowledge about warfare and intelligence gathering. There are scores of books written about how adept the Russians were about the fundamentals and advanced nuances of espionage. One small portion of those fundamentals that directly correlates to Gray Man principles is a numbered list known as the Moscow Rules.

The Soviet Syllabus (aka The Moscow Rules):

1. Assume nothing.
2. Never go against your gut.
3. Everyone is potentially under opposition control.
4. Do not look back; you are never completely alone.
5. Go with the flow, blend in.
6. Vary your pattern and stay within your cover.
7. Lull them into a sense of complacency.
8. Do not harass the opposition.
9. Pick the time and place for action.
10. Keep your options open.[1,2]

Below is a summary of each rule:

1.   Assume nothing.

It is best not to assume unless there is no other alternative due to a lack of concrete evidence to support a position or decision. Assumptions become the greatest enemy of large groups. Making a wrong assumption about a group may mean missing the opportunity for two leveled headed, or at least willing, people to work out differences or peacefully debate. The old expression about the word assume is quite relevant. Deconstructed, the word *assume* appears as ASS/U/ME. Meaning when you assume, it has the remarkable potential for making an **ass** of *u* and **me**.

2.   Never go against your gut.

We all have had that feeling of something not being right or a little off. Yet, we have proceeded only to discover the manifestation of we chose to ignore. Most of the time, it produces only an inconvenience. Other times it produces agonizing relationship problems or financial difficulties. In extreme cases, it produces life-altering or life-ending results that we can only regret and cannot change.

3.   Everyone is potentially under opposition control.

This seems a bit of an oxymoron within the context of Rule #1. But, it has more to do with trusting and vetting potential allies. It also references the importance of the principles of Selectivity and Suppression discussed in *Conversational Camouflage* regarding OPSEC (Operations Security).

4. Don't look back; you are never completely alone.

Currently, with all the surveillance and security monitoring in every place where we conduct business and visit throughout our daily routines, this statement has never been more true. Any attempt to completely avoid detection or surveillance, including self-imposed confinement, is considered very suspicious behavior. Even the in-home technology from Smartphones and the plethora of in-home wireless connectivity products from alarm systems, televisions, appliances, and thermostats make staying surveillance-free a nearly impossible endeavor. To eliminate all surveillance sources, one must make the choice and effort to be virtually technology-free.

5. Go with the flow, blend in.

This rule is the very heart and soul of the Gray Man. You must be able to blend in. More importantly, you must learn or relearn to go with the established flow of the current culture and baseline. It is also a lot harder than it seems when you add other factors such as having to have (and exercise) patience with people who walk slower, pay less attention, and show little or no regard for others around them. Remember also, that the rules of vehicular travel do not necessarily translate to pedestrian travel. Pedestrians will overtake from either side and not maintain any type of lane discipline. They brake without warning and turn without signaling.

6. Vary your pattern and stay within your cover.

Just like Rule #5, this too, is one of the major foundations of the Gray Man. It is important to vary your routine and reduce your visible profile as much as possible. Your cover is the movement of your fellow citizens. Move within groups and move within shadows when they make themselves available.

7. Lull them into a sense of complacency.

Getting people to let their guard down while maintaining your own vigilance is sometimes difficult to accomplish. This usually depends on how well crafted and executed your pretext or cover story is. You would be surprised at how well a smile will disarm even the most vigilant person. If it did not work, con-men, spies, and police officers would not do it.

8. Do not harass the opposition.

If you are trying to stay under the radar, being antagonistic is not going to aid you and make it easier to influence others in becoming your ally. Nor does it generate any sympathy for your cause. The recent riots and looting in America are deeply resented by many Americans, with few citizens able to empathize with the events that preceded the protests *after* they turned violent and destructive. Everything about the Gray Man must be centered around self-control and the ability to relinquish one's ego to deescalate tense or hostile situations. The cooler head must prevail.

9. Pick the time and place for action.

If the situation worsens to the point where physical conflict is eminent, you still must try to control the situation. Delaying or expediting a justifiable, necessary and reasonable response to ensure better positioning, passive (security cameras) or active (individuals) witnesses, reduction of objects used against you, minimize property damage, and/or open an avenue of egress and escape.

10. Keep your options open.

There are a whole handful or more clichés and proverbial sayings that easily relate to this rule, but here are just a few: Do not put all your eggs in one basket and do not burn your bridges. Always leave yourself a way out, do not paint yourself into a corner. The more you keep this concept in your head, the more likely you are to avoid danger or conflict.

This also includes on relying too much on Gray Man skills or tactics. As much as I like the subject of the Gray Man and its relationship to camouflage and concealment, the tactic cannot and will not work for every person. I cannot be a used car salesman and promise you that this tactic, "runs like a dream" or "has plenty of life left in her." It is not ethical or honest to make such a careless statement. As much as writing on the subject is my bread and butter, the reality of the Gray Man is that once several people in an area try to avoid standing out, they are going to. They will make going gray the *observable* new normal simply by trying to implement or over-implement it in a conflict area.

PRACTICAL SKILL-SET:

The adage, "A picture is worth a thousand words" provides the backdrop for the development and strengthening of Gray Man principles in this exercise.

Keeping in mind the previous Soviet Syllabus section, view several randomly selected pictures from the internet that feature groups of people in various locations, times, etc. You may wish to have someone else select the photos for you. Address each rule and apply it to what you see in the photo. As you do this, focus on the following "How's" of blending in often used by Gray Man practitioners.

In each scenario, how would you:

1. Manipulate the perception of others.
2. Mimic behavior.
3. Match/mirror the baseline.
4. Master self-control.

Finally, how would you implement your choices? Focusing and using the **S.A.F.E.** acronym, described as **S**ubtle, **A**stute, **F**inesse, and **E**fficient.

Subtle – How unnoticed could you expect to implement your blending efforts?

Astute – How much scholarly confidence could you exude to implement your blending efforts?

Finesse – How much charisma and charm could you generate to implement your blending efforts?

Efficient – How fast and accurate could you implement your blending efforts?

Sources and Citations:

[1] *Mendez, Antonio & Jonna, with Baglio, Matt, The Moscow Rules: The Secret CIA Tactics That Helped America Win the Cold War, Public Affairs Publishing, May 2019*
[2] https://en.wikipedia.org/wiki/The_Moscow_rules

There is significant evidence as to why gray and other neutral colors invoke the subliminal and emotional responses they do. Invoke probably is not the best word because it infers a strong response, but neutral colors generally create feelings of relaxation and calm. Of course, not everyone responds the same way to colors based upon personal preference, experience, and both passive and active association. There is much more information on the subject of color psychology that I am neither qualified to discuss nor willing to delve into within the scope of this work, but nevertheless, it is a fascinating topic that plays a significant role in urban camouflage and concealment.

Shade

There are over 500 shades of gray the human eye can detect.[1] When asked how to describe one of these many gradients, people will offer generic descriptions of intensity from light to dark. Generally, they are not concerned with name as one would find on a paint swatch or the Pantone designator used by the print industry. The shade intensity come more into play as the individual's perception and interpretation of the opposite colors of the visible spectrum (white and black) is introduced into an environment.

Symbology

Color symbology has been around for millennia. Part of the reason the Gray Man principle works, is its non-committal to the long-standing color symbology associated with black and white. White is seen in many Western cultures as being pure, innocent, virginal, and morally good, with black being regarded as ominous, sinister, and morally evil. However, even within our own culture, those color attributes are not without exceptions.

The attributes change with context. If you say someone's soul is black, you are inferring that person is evil. But, if you describe their hair color as black, that is a genetic trait that is unchangeable without the assistance of time or the manipulation through hair coloring techniques and products. Even further, if you say someone's suit or dress is black, it speaks of formality, style, and elegance. In the examples above, a black soul would be regarded as negative, black hair would be neutral, and black formal attire would be considered positive.

When gray is introduced, the observer must make more assumptions as to the color interpretation and must wait for more information or behavior to occur to make judgements or decisions on the observed person's intent.

For example, look at the country of India. India has a rich culture which is abundantly clear in the use of vibrant colors for their clothing materials. There are so many bright shades of yellows, reds, and oranges that choosing a color like white would not only stand out; but could convey a subliminal cultural message which may be detrimental to your attempt to not draw attention to yourself. In India, only widows are allowed to wear white and is also associated with funerals or other ceremonies denoting the death of a family member.[5]

Another color typically associated as neutral in the West would be light shades of brown. However, in India, brown earth tones such as ochre symbolize wealth and grandeur.[5] Obviously, if you are trying to keep a low profile, this color would have the opposite effect. Keep in mind, color symbology can also change in certain geographic regions, even within the same country.

Modernization
Colors of pre-industrial era
Colors of modernity
Colors of postmodernism

Globalization
National colors
Political colors
Ideological colors
Religious colors

Economic development
Colors expressing wealth
Non-color expressing wealth

New generations
Colors in youth culture
Colors in popular culture
Colors in consumer brands

Minorities
Ethnic colors
Religious colors
Linguistic color meanings

Gender roles
Gender-bound colors

Mantua-Kommonen, Kirsi. (2014). Provenance of cultural color meanings - towards a conceptual framework.

Stereotypes

I mentioned stereotypes and how they relate to the implementation of Gray Man tactics in my first Gray Man book. To say that some of the feedback and reviews were mixed would be an understatement.   People have strong opinions and oftentimes intolerant of the opinions of others. Even in my attempt to explain how and why stereotypes are used and manipulated in some circumstances, some saw it as a glorification and justification for racism and hatred. My motive was nowhere close to the allegations hurled in my direction. The extent to which their bias was revealed is ironically laughable.

So again, bear in mind that I am not promoting or condoning these things in an illegal, criminal manner.   I am, however, acknowledging the existence of stereotypes and bias to determine a level of profiling that is lawfully done and generally accepted for the purpose of personal safety.   This is the basis for what is known as pretexting, the development and implementation of false identity for the purpose of infiltration, exfiltration, and moving about without or with limited opposition in a Non-Permissive Environment (NPE).

The color gray and its varying tones and shades portray and create emotional responses just as every other color the human eye can differentiate. The reason why the Gray Man is called "gray" has more to do with the psychological stereotypes associated with it than any other reason. Certain colors based upon our culture, faith, ethnicity, and our experiences can create powerful bias and associations. Whether those colors are interpreted as good or bad, welcome or unpleasant, are subjective to the individual. To the point, the Gray Man principle is all about manipulating and exploiting other people's preconceived notions and expectations when observed by them. It dictates how we present ourselves to have the desired effects of concealment based upon the exploitation of the color stereotypes.

Associations, representations, and emotions that may be invoked by the color gray:[1,2,3,4]

Intellect
Knowledge
Wisdom
Long-lasting
Classic
Sleek
Refined
Indifferent
Lifeless
Isolated
Dignified
Balanced
Professional
Efficiency
Conservative
Authority
Detachment
Lacking character
Neutral
Unsettling
Creates expectations
Non-involvement
Non-committal
Pessimism
Practical
Formal
Quiet
Timelessness

Depress energy
Maturity
Compromise
Dependable
Boring
Lonely
Basic
Colorless
Rigid
Good
Unimaginative
Reserved
Smart
Innocent
Reflective
Calming
Fresh
Gloomy
Unemotional
Detached
Avoiding attention
Depression
Stabilizing
Frustration
Control
Lacking initiative
Solid
Reliable
Peaceful
Relaxing
Soothing

Sad
Indecisive
Insightful advice
Uninteresting
Dull
Traditional
Serious

You will have noticed that a few of the listed words contradict with other words on the list. Add to that the different color meanings and symbology within other countries and cultures, and you can begin to understand why there would be times and places where the color gray is not going to provide the desired anonymity.

You will have also noticed there are words that are clearly not what we want from a situational sense/awareness point of view. While it is clear some of the words have a deep association to the color gray, some of the emotions and attitudes are not conducive to the way we portray ourselves in public when using Gray Man tactics. Just as a few examples, you would not want to display an appearance of frustration, indecisiveness, or be unsettled.

Style

To muddy the waters even further, when you add the style and fashion factor into the mix, it can create more assumptions than you intended to convey. Style is normally a subjective expression or extension of one's preferences and personality. The problem arises when a collective generalization regarding an article of clothing becomes detrimental based upon the application of the social labelling theory.

As a benign example, let us say you visit a town where everyone owns a black leather jacket. The most common is a conservative-looking casual leather jacket. Rather than buying a new jacket, you pull out your old black leather biker jacket and give it no further attention beyond the two qualifiers of being both black in color and the material being leather. Unbeknownst to you, the town does not hold bikers in high regard, so when you walk down the street, you are met with looks of suspicion, disapproval, and even contempt. Therefore, context is so important regarding Gray Man tactics.

Speculation/Suspicions

There is a fine line between trusting your gut and making reckless assumptions about people and their ability to become potential threats to your safety. Nobody likes to be met with suspicion, but if someone's behavior warrants it, scrutinize the living daylights out of them until you are satisfied that they are of little or no threat. In today's world, people will get offended at the slightest thing, so if your safety is put into question, someone else's feeling take a back seat and they can go pound sand for all I care. Sorry, but I am not sorry. Not even a little bit.

You should also remember that there are cultures where it is normal and/or acceptable to stare. Being mindful of where and when this may be applicable means you are less likely to be offended when on the receiving end of a stare. It also gives you some freedom to establish motive and behavioral intent when you apply the technique.

PRACTICAL SKILL-SET:

Pick a different city, a different state, and a different country where you would most likely visit or find yourself living, answering the following questions:

5. What is the median income of that area? Do you exceed it or fall below it?
6. How different is the language, also taking into consideration other factors such as slang, accents, dialects, etc.
7. How do the native inhabitants view outsiders? Are they aggressive or aloof?
8. What is the predominant religious belief? If your beliefs differ, how do the current residents respond/react to those differences?
9. What is the popular political persuasion? Does it conform or contradict your own political leadings?
10. What is the average education level? Is your level of education higher or lower?
11. What is the baseline regarding the typically measured and recorded demographic metrics such as age, gender, health, race, and ethnicity?
12. Where and when do people congregate and their reasons for doing so? Example: Do teens hang out at the skate parks or shopping malls? Do they have favorite places to gather?
13. When people gather, what activities are taking place? Are they individually performed and motivated or corporate and collective?
14. What cultural differences and expectations are displayed? Is there a high level of conformity expected/demanded?
15. When does the area become most active and populated? Is it busier during the day or at night? At dawn or at dusk? During the week or on weekends?
16. What types of laws and ordinances are in place and how strict are those laws enforced? Are people armed? What are the crime statistics for the area?

Use the following space below to write some additional considerations and questions to ask.

Sources and Citations:

[1]http://www.riptapparel.com/blog/category/cool-infographics/
#.UQmhkejjebE, as listed on original infographic, but currently 404 not
found.
[2]http://www.color-meanings.com
[3]http://www.crystal-cure.com/color-meanings.html
[4]http://www.GRAF1X.com
[5]https://www.sensationalcolor.com/symbolic-colors-india/

As the chapter title implies, there are significant advantages and disadvantages in having routines as it applies to Gray Man tactics. While it is highly advantageous from a time management and productivity standpoint to utilize routines, they can be easily compromised by complacency and the boredom created by repetitive activities.

Schedules

We are creatures of habit and lust after efficiency. The mantra of "Work smarter, not harder" is repeatedly hammered into our consciousness. It does not always sink in, but it is repeated enough where most people in American culture have heard it. Because of that drive for efficiency and to take full advantage of our time, we often use scheduling to make sure tasks are not forgotten.

I am not saying people should abandon the use of schedules and routines. In our culture, it is almost impossible. Especially when our lives revolve around our jobs, children's school, extracurricular activities, making sure we get home in time to take the dog out, cooking dinner, picking up the dry-cleaning...the list goes on and on.

We make schedules because, inherently as human beings, we like predictability. We place expectations on people and things to be where they say they will be or do what they are designed to do. Nobody likes pulling up to the school yard to pick up their child to find the child not at the pick-up zone. It instantly creates a moment of panic in the heart of a parent. Likewise, no one approaches the office copy machine with a cavalier, Russian Roulette attitude and desirous thrill of "Will it print or not". We expect it to work and print our document.

Surveillance

When your life offers no variation beyond the day of the week, you are going to have a harder time implementing Gray Man skills when those skills are needed. An established routine is much easier to predict and provide surveillance, rather than one that has multiple variations. Granted, good surveillance teams will adeptly adjust their procedures and plans to keep tabs on you. But having a concrete routine makes their job a lot easier. Criminals do the same type of behaviors when they "case a joint" or target a victim.

You may be able to recall several movies where a person of interest has their daily routine "narrated" by the intelligence gatherer of a group and he or she exposes the potential weaknesses and vulnerabilities of the surveilled person to others within the group. In much the same way, a good majority of our own lives and those of our loved ones could be scrutinized and exploited the same way.

Set-Up Scenarios

An effective way to break up routines is to implement impromptu drills and scenarios. These types of events cause minimal interruption when compared to the potential problems encountered during real-life events. It is much easier to have an alert tone set up on your phone notifying you to self-initiate an emergency evacuation drill to leave a building rather than try to navigate through panicked people trying to exit in an unrehearsed frenzy.

Running drills allows you to prepare ahead of time, have PACE and/or SPACE procedures in place (refer to Chapter One), and avoid indecision and panic in an emergency or crisis. It is often said that people revert to their lowest level of training during crisis, so it is paramount that you train and practice to maintain skills and can faithfully execute plans and protocols to remove yourself and loved ones out of harm's way.

PRACTICAL SKILL-SET:

Below is a list of several different activities you can vary or alter throughout you day or week in an effort to break up routines and predicted habits. Obviously, there will blocks of time where you will be required to be at a certain place like work and some things you may not be able to alter such as break times or lunch. However, many of the activities offer great flexibility and cost little or no money to do.

- Wake up 10, 20, or 30 minutes early.
- Take a different route to work.
- Take a different form of transportation to work.
- Use different accessories like ball caps to alter your look.
- Consciously change your gait and stride when walking.
- Alternate between strong/weak hand when carrying items.
- Ask a colleague or spouse to identify verbal crutches and go-to phrases. Then work on replacing or refraining from those words.
- During your lunch break, watch people instead of scrolling through your smartphone.
- Change your workout times and exercises/activities.
- If not enrolled in a gym, change where you exercise.
- Run emergency evacuation drills from your home, work, and frequently visited locations.
- Choose a random vehicle, follow it for 5-10 minutes and mentally recon as much information as you can.
- Visit different restaurants or order something different from your "usual" selection.

Use the provided lines on the following page to come up with your own ideas to change up your daily routine and schedules:

Sources and Citations:

[1]   https://www.thetravel.com/10-places-where-eye-contact-is-not-recommended-10-places-where-the-locals-are-friendly/

Savvy is not a word we use much in today's modern English language, but we should. Google's dictionary defines savvy as "shrewdness and practical knowledge, the ability to make good judgements." The online Merriam-Webster dictionary defines savvy as, "having or showing perception, comprehension, or shrewdness especially in practical matters" and "Practical know-how."

There is not a single book, manual, or magazine article discussing the Gray Man principles that does not mention situational awareness. The two subjects are married together. So, when looking at the above definition of the word savvy, it should come as no surprise that a useful acronym should start with situational awareness.

SAVVY is acronym for **S**ituational **A**wareness, **V**ision, **V**igilance, wh**Y**?

SITUATIONAL AWARENESS

As discussed in my earlier works, as well as other books available on the subject, most people understand Situational Awareness to simply mean being aware of one's surroundings and environment. The "How-To" will be explained in the upcoming section.

VISION

Your eyes are your greatest asset regarding the perceiving of danger, interpreting stimuli, and orientating yourself to your immediate location and towards your desired destination. Vision is also having the foresight to plan routes and the ability to visualize and construct a course of action for a different number of scenarios.

VIGILANCE

Your ability to remain vigilant ultimately determines your safety. As soon as one or more attention saboteurs emerge, your attempts at vigilance become difficult to maintain. I will mention attention saboteurs later in Chapter 7 in the Seven Deadly Sins of Situational Awareness section.

WHY?

"Why" is your justification for taking the necessary precautions to safeguard your life and employ Gray Man skills to begin with. You have purposefully and soberly acknowledged the many potential dangers you may face in a particular environment and have taken the appropriate precautions, learned defensive skills, and proactively increased your awareness to avoid those potential dangers.

The ABC's of Situational Awareness

In addition to all the sensory stimuli we receive, our brains instantly begin construction on a frame of reference for every situation we encounter. This frame of reference is influenced and heavily contingent upon the following factors:

Situational Alerts and Anomalies
Situational Bias and Behavior
Situational Context and Cognition
Situational Demands and Deviations
Situational Experience and Expectations

Increasing Situational Sense and Awareness

Oftentimes, those new to the concept of situational awareness and those wishing to increase that awareness are met with the response, "Just be more aware of your surroundings." When people ask how to go about increasing their ability to sense and interpret what is going on around them, they need to be given tools and instruction. Many times, people already "in the know" do a disservice to those legitimately wanting and needing to know how by not clearly articulating what that looks like or how to assist in the development of better perception/detection skills and habits. Most admonishments are akin to "keep your head on a swivel" or "get your face out of your phone", but newcomers need and deserve better instruction than that.

As both practitioner and instructor, I have an obligation to ensure students know how to apply the concepts and techniques I teach. Some of this instruction requires practical, hands-on and in-person instruction. Some of it can be learned through instruction and seminars. The bottom line is to meet students at their level of understanding and build from there. The result of this self-imposed mandate has culminated into twelve analytical and actionable ways to increase situational awareness. By proactively engaging in the following twelve steps, the reader should be able to increase their situational awareness efforts.

1. **Acknowledge risks and potential dangers.** The first step to being more aware is acknowledging the need for increased awareness arising from the present dangers and risks in the world around you.

2. **Substantiate/verify risks against local law enforcement records and reporting.** We should neither be naïve nor paranoid about the actual dangers present where we live, work, and play. As an informed citizen, you should try to gather the most accurate information and crime reports for the areas you frequent and conduct your daily life.

3. **Define your personal space requirements and expectations.** Every person is different, and their unique definition and perception of personal space will vary. If you are the type of person who is introverted, hates loud noises, and dislikes being tightly packed into confined spaces with others, your level of anxiety is going to be greater in a dance club than a grocery store.

4. **Identify actions that trigger your suspicion or anxiety.** The key word here is actions. Actions and behavior should predominantly arouse suspicions; not personal appearances, features, or any other attribute that can be construed as

discriminatory or used to profile someone else in a negative manner. While it is impossible and extremely naïve to expect everyone to not have bias and stereotypes or make some generalizations, this should not be the norm for most people.

5. **Create a risk mitigation/contingency plan.** The best plan is to avoid the places that potentially put you at greater risk or are generally uncomfortable. However, you may need to travel to a business meeting or conference in a distant city. You may have to stay in a hotel or motel. You have no way of knowing the potential behavior of the other guests.

6. **Obtain and practice the skills necessary to effectively execute your plan.** Some of the skills that increase your situational awareness do not require any financial cost to practice. Using window glass and flat surfaces to monitor other people is a great way to use your surroundings to their full advantage. Other skills like self-defense and weapons handling will require enrollment and regular attendance in classes to gain proficiency.

7. **Adjust or modify the physiological saboteurs (i.e., diet, exercise, sleep, alcohol consumption) to maximize your ability to pay closer attention.** What we put into our bodies can greatly affect our cognitive ability to recognize danger and forces our senses to either work harder to detect potential threats, degrades their efficiency, or even worse, shut down, making us completely vulnerable.

8. **Turn off all unnecessary electronic and technology distractions.** I cannot beat this into people's consciousness enough. The modern smartphone, with all its features and

applications, is NOT a life-support device. At best, it is a life-enhancing device. But, if you cannot put your mobile device away for fifteen minutes or constantly feel the need to check for notifications, you may find yourself on the receiving end of a different kind of life-support device. Remember, a person intently glued to their phone screen is a victim that a criminal both prays to meet and preys upon.

9. **Avoid multi-tasking when possible.** Trying to do too many things at the same time opens us up to the possibility of losing focus or paying too much attention to a specific task. Granted, some people can multi-task, but I have witnessed far too often that quality of work is sacrificed for the sake of quantity.

10. **Use the Pan-Tilt-Zoom method of aware observation rather than the "head on a swivel" technique.** As I previously wrote in *Situational Sense*, the Pan-Tilt-Zoom method involves slowly looking from left to right and right to left, up and down, and then zooming in (focusing) on anything that looks out of place when compared to the baseline surroundings. Relying only on side-to-side rotation looks too much like Robocop.

11. **Give yourself time and room to move.** By giving yourself time and space to move when dangers start to manifest helps provide some more reaction time to locate avenues of escape. If you do not give yourself enough time to get from one appointment to the next, you may end up selecting a faster, but less-safe, route. Giving yourself more time allows for unforeseen delays. I have never heard of anyone being punished or chastised for being early.

12. **Warn others.** Part of the obligation of being situationally aware sometimes places you in the position of warning others of an arising danger. It would be morally irresponsible and reprehensible to allow someone to walk into a dangerous situation. While we cannot make every person heed our warnings, at least our conscience can be clear that the effort was made to divert others from the same threat. However, the final decision to proceed or take a detour is laid squarely on the shoulders of the recipient.

What's Your SAT Score?

This is not a question about aptitude to enroll in a college or university. In this context, SAT is an acronym for **S**uspicion/**A**nxiety **T**riggers. I hazard a guess that everyone has certain triggers. Anyone claiming otherwise is not human. Having and knowing your personal SATs does not mean you will fall to pieces, nor does it mean you will rise to the challenge when confronted with those triggers. However, the likelihood of overcoming them when your life is on the line is better if you know what you are looking for in the first place.

This is not intended to be a diagnosis of bona fide phobias and medically recognized anxiety. Nor is intended to make light or marginalize someone's intense feelings about certain types of situations or things that may induce genuine feelings of panic or fear.

When quickly researching for a brief overview of the topic of fear, most of what I found was presented from the medical and mental health standpoint of diagnosable phobias. By definition, phobias are irrational fears under most circumstances. What I plan to discuss are some of the basic triggers and circumstances that tend to produce doubt, worry, or anxiety when they occur.

For example, on a scale of 1 to 10 with one being the lowest and ten being the highest, breaking glass registers at an 8 or 9 for me. I absolutely hate it. It is sometimes unavoidable, and accidents happen. I am not sure the anxiety is due to being yelled at as a child for breaking a glass item or understand the potential for lacerations from shattered glass. Now the complete opposite happens when glass shatters in a movie. It maybe registers as a 2 or 3 on the scale. It does increase slightly to 4 or 5 when scenes depicting the removal of glass from the skin. I still cringe watching *Die Hard* when John McClane is pulling glass from his feet. I know it is fake, but the imagery still triggers a bit of anxiety.

It is important to remember that it is okay to have suspicion/anxiety triggers. They are a defense mechanism and early warning system. Without them, you could unknowingly walk into any number of hazardous and dangerous situations.

PRACTICAL SKILL-SET:

Carefully review the previous two sections, Increasing Situational Sense and Awareness and What's Your SAT Score, specifically focusing on points 4, 5, and 6. Use the space below to identify the things listed in those points as they are applicable to you and your unique situation.

____

____

____

____

____

____

____

____

____

____

____

____

Once you have identified those things, any trigger you feel is or could become a potential barrier needs to be changed or managed.

One thing people tend to overlook is the fact that even when we are not speaking, we are communicating. The crossing of arms, the positioning of feet, how and where we glance are all manifestations of our internal thought processes through body language. We are always communicating, even if there is no one present to observe and interpret. Therefore, when in the presence of others, we need to be cognizant of what and how we are communicating.

In the beginning of the book, you will have noticed the quotation from Stevie Ray Vaughan's song, *Couldn't Stand the Weather*. It seemed appropriate in today's world. There is an obvious and ominous storm brewing on the horizon. The wind has picked up and the rain has started falling in many places. About the only thing one can talk about with causing offense is the weather. As a result, I began formulating some acronyms that can be used as code for communicating with others concerning the situations and scenarios you may face.

In the following examples of coded communication, there is no sliding scale of escalation, as far as priority or immediacy is concerned. Nor does it infer or assume any level of severity as the list progresses. The words relate to weather conditions, as it seems to be the only subject that can be discussed without offending anyone.

Talk About the Weather

Just as we would unlikely leave our homes without having some idea of the potential weather we may encounter throughout the day or for the length of a journey, we do not want to be unprepared for other anomalies we have no control over. The best we can do is avoid areas altogether or have a plan and tools available to reduce our exposure.

This is not the only way to incorporate some OPSEC related code language into your Gray Man practices. It may not be the best way for you, either. This is merely an example of how one can insert seemingly benign, coded text into a practicable skillset. You could use any number of things that work for you: animals, movie characters, movie quotes, whatever you can remember.

WET – (**W**arranted **E**xternal **T**hreats)

WIND – (**W**eaponized/**I**mprovised **N**uclear **D**evice)

FOG – (**F**oreign **O**pposition/**G**angs)

ICE – (**I**ncited **C**risis **E**vents)

HAIL – (**H**ome **A**ttack/**I**nvasion **L**arceny)

SLEET – (**S**low **L**aw **E**nforcement **E**ngagemen**T**)

RAIN – (**R**iots **A**narchy **I**nsurrectio**N**)

MIST – (**M**ass **I**njuries **S**ignificant **T**rauma)

SNOW – (**S**ystems or **S**ervices **N**on-**O**perational/**W**ar)

Try to establish patterns with length of words, rhyming words, related words, etc. Common sense should dictate the avoidance of words that have negative connotations, meanings, or would obviously be picked up in search algorithms as buzzwords by DHS, FBI, CIA, etc., such as BOMB, BANG, or GUN.

Here are a few other examples of benign or mostly neutral words and a relevant acronym to use. Of course, you do not have to use the same acronyms.

CABS – **C**riminal **A**ctivity/**B**ehavior **S**uspicious

CARS – **C**onflicts **A**narchy **R**iots **S**hutdowns

TABS – **T**error **A**ttacks **B**ombing **S**edition

These words do not bring much attention to themselves. However, these words could also spell out SCAB, SCAR, and STAB, respectively. Those choices are a bit more provocative and could possibly bring some unwanted attention. This type of communication only works within a small group of people who have been briefed on the coded words and their coded meanings. For instance, let us use the word CARS. One might ask, "Did you see any cars today?" The response could be a make or model correlated to the correct letter, "Yes, I saw a Suburban." Because Suburban starts with the letter S, the associated letter in the acronym references Shutdown, preserving both the overt and covert context.

Safety Words

Safety words or passwords are often used with children. If an unfamiliar adult approaches the child not knowing the proper password, the child flees to a designated haven like back inside a school, store, or police station. The same concept applies to adults.

Speech

When discussing verbal communication, there are several factors that affect one's ability to effectively communicate and still manage to reduce or minimize stimuli on the part of the message recipient. These factors are:

Language
Lexicon
Pronunciation
Annunciation
Inflection
Tone
Innuendo
Slang
Accent
Dialect

Mastering the English language is difficult; even for native or first language speakers. However, those who learn English as a second or third language have a far more difficult time. There are so many nuances, dual-meanings, contextual differences, colloquialisms, homonyms, and alternate spellings that it deserves much more empathy to people to whom English is a second language.

Likewise, most Americans who are now second or third generation removed from immigrants have a significant reduction or even no second language skills beyond what is offered within the realm of foreign language electives in school.

Silent Speech

Silent Speech is simply body language; non-verbal cues and signals that communicate attitudes and feelings that may not be recognizable or may be intentionally hidden during verbal dialogue. While I am not a body language expert, I can provide some simple clues to look for when talking with or observing other people. As an example, let us consider a person traveling on a public train. When they get close to their intended stop, they may:

Shift – Start to move their eyes to indicators or focus on visual/audio announcements. They may shift their body weight more frequently in preparation to move.

Sort – A passenger getting ready to exit will sort and gather their belongings.

Stand/Shuffle – A passenger may stand and make their way towards a door as space avails itself with small, shuffling steps.

Vehicular Body Language

People also communicate non-verbally with their vehicles, so it is important to address some of the ways people converse with each other.

Signaling – Using one's turn signal is one of the best ways to communicate your intentions while driving. As good as an indicator (pun intended) is, there are some who frequently fail to use the device, resulting in other signaling from aggravated drivers in the forms of various offensive hand gestures, horn blasts, and shouted obscenities.

Slowing/Stopping – Braking tells others behind you of your need or desire to slow down, turn, or stop and demands their obligation to heed and comply to avoid a collision. It is sometimes used in a passive-aggressive manner to warn others behind you to slow down or give more distance between vehicles.

Swerving – Swerving almost always carries with it the notion of inattentive or impaired driving. However, it can indicate an obstruction in the road that has suddenly appeared, that now allows those travelling behind the swerving vehicle the opportunity to avoid the obstacle slowly and safely.

Speeding – Speeding translates into impatience, regardless of any justification given for it. While there are some clear safety reasons for speed limits, I, like many others, recognize that the casual enforcement is linked more with the generation of revenue within a jurisdiction than with actual safety matters, which would require stricter enforcement.

When discussing communications, we are also talking about how to control conversation and persuade escalation and de-escalation, as well as influencing others for the purposes of rendering aid, providing information, or even turning a blind eye to an act they have witnessed us or someone else commit. One way we can do this is by using four communication styles to influence the listener. Brady Pesola, a preparedness and personal security consultant, who is known as gray.man.project on several social media platforms such as Instagram, Tik Tok, and Facebook refer to these styles as the "Four Horsemen" of manipulation.

These characteristics are Charisma, Humor, Kindness, and Empathy. In one of his Instagram/Tik Tok posts, Pesola goes on to state there is a proper sequence and timing that is situationally dependent upon the type of person and what you are trying to convince them to do. However, when looked at each characteristic individually, you can see how they might be effective.

Charisma is one of those personality traits which seems like either you have it, or you do not. The best way to portray this is with confidence, attitude, and positive body language signals such as smiling, showing open palms, facing the listener, etc.

Humor is the wild card of the bunch because of all the different varieties of humor out there. Trying to guess accurately whether someone likes pun-based humor, dead pan, or even dark humor is challenging without having some prior knowledge or relationship with the individual. Situational humor is tricky as well. Some people in stressful situations might otherwise enjoy quips and witty sarcasm, but the timing and circumstances prevent them from responding favorably to you.

You can never go too wrong with kindness, but that kindness should not be naively distributed without constraint or vigilance. The late, famous evangelist Billy Graham used to say, "People don't care what you know, until they know you care." There is a lot of truth in that statement and by showing or offering a bit of kindness through a helping hand often provides the "in". It often subconsciously plants the seed of reciprocated obligation in the mind of the recipient. They may offer money or provide you with a bit of information you need.

Empathy is the icing on the cake, so to speak. If you can apply the first three but cannot manage to relate to the individual or attempt to maintain a perceived level of dominance or superiority over them, you are not going to get far at all. You really do have to put yourself in their shoes or visualize how you would respond in their situation.

Pesola does not sugarcoat the purpose and objectives for the use of these communications tactics, but he also goes on to emphasize to use common sense as well as having a correctly calibrated moral compass. In other words, do not go around doing this to talk old ladies out of their pension money or intentionally defraud someone. To which, I agree.

For ease in remembering, you could rearrange the letters to form the acronym, CHEK.

Scaling (escalation and de-escalation)

For any Gray Man practices to be truly effective, individuals must possess not simply good communication skills, but excellent communication skills. You must know how and when to use the concept of scaling; either the escalation or de-escalation of a situation using your verbal skills. There should never be any rush to circumvent verbal skills for the sake of implementing violence in its place. While there are situations warranting an immediate violent defensive response, there should be vocal, verbal communication coinciding with those actions.

Regardless of the other person's intention to obey your commands or engage in dialogue, prudence and case law have determined this to be necessary to establish self-defense as a legal argument and defense. It may not to keep you out of the defendant's seat, but it may help avoid a conviction and a prison sentence.

We can see in society today the severe diminishing of civility regarding the way we talk and communicate with people. This is quite evident on the myriad of social media platforms. Despite this overwhelming lack of decorum and civility online, the reality of in-person verbal interaction demands a greater reliance on self-control, accuracy, brevity, and conciseness.

Anyone who possesses a concealed carry weapon (CCW) license or has a knowledge of law enforcement tactics understands the significant weight and focus put on the issue of the escalation and use of force. It is important to keep up to date with your state's current use of force/deadly force laws.

Sharing

Much of what is written about Gray Man tactics could be mistaken as a lone wolf or a one-person application, but that would be untrue. First, because of the sheer numbers of those interested in the subject, how we share relevant information with other practitioners is important. Humans are societal creatures, and despite how our current society is displaying itself, we still need each other. Friends and family still heavily rely upon us to pass along vital information crucial to our long-term safety and survival. If sharing were not important, there would be no videos, books, magazine articles, or seminars offered at varying price points to help us. All the knowledge you and I have accumulated does not benefit anyone else unless we share it or make it available to others.

Scouting

A big part of successful Gray Man tactics is scouting and reconnaissance. It would be both practically and tactically unwise to go into any environment without first knowing some basic information about the area. People pragmatically do it all the time when planning vacations and holidays. Most people do not like surprises; especially when the purposes of such trips are for relaxing and enjoyment. Anything that can potentially spoil those goals are identified, contingencies planned, and hopefully avoided.

I usually like to use a much more detailed and comprehensive list of features and observational points when conducting my own in-depth scouting and recon. Since it is not always necessary or expedient to use that list for quick, preliminary scouting, I use the SALUTE report developed by the US army.

SALUTE is an acronym for:

Size – This describes the number or quantity of people being observed. Those familiar with military units such as squad, patrol, platoon, battalion, company, division will probably report group sizes in this manner, but it may be easier and clearer to report a simple number, such as 25.

Activity – This describes what the individuals are doing. They could be walking, running, or just standing. Positioning and order can be used to ascertain any leadership hierarchy present. One individual addressing others who are in formations such as columns/rows, semi-circles/arcs, or a perimeter around them would be potentially in charge.

Location – This describes where the activity and individuals are currently located. It is important to be as accurate as possible and orient their position.

Unit/Uniform – This describes an organization, possibly identified through the issuance or donning of a uniform. This can also be an indicator of how trained, organized, and dedicated to the carrying out of the observed activity.

Time – This describes the local time at which the activity and individuals were initially observed. SITREPs (Situation Reports) would provide further updates as necessary in terms of forward chronology.

Equipment – This describes any weapons, support and communications gear the observed individuals are using or have in their possession to assist in carrying out the observed activity.

A secondary reporting method is the SALT report. It is slightly shorter and eliminates the unit/uniform and equipment portions. That is not to say those elements are not important, but in terms of quick reporting and specificity, some of the observables may be more difficult to accurately report. For instance, a specific weapon system might cause hesitation in the attempt to accurately describe and identify it. Another example would be having to accurately identify a camouflage pattern on a uniform. These examples do not mean that further questions and clarification will not be asked for and expected. Typically, the receiver of the report will ask for supporting evidence and information, so the SALT and SALUTE reports are merely a starting point for building a more comprehensive intelligence report.

PRACTICAL SKILL-SET:

<u>**Activity 1:**</u>

Develop a list of code words or phrases with a training group, your family members, neighborhood watch group, etc. that you can use to communicate certain events, scenarios, or procedures.

Common words can be used as acronyms to describe people or situations. For example, the word **COFFEE** could mean **C**omply, **O**bey, **F**ollow, **F**all In, **E**mbrace, **E**nslavement. In a simple question, one could ask, "Do you like coffee?" Those knowing the cipher would give the correct response. Their response would be independent or unrelated to their actual like or dislike of coffee. There are multiple ways that one could extrapolate this out further, but you get the general idea.

Using coded language will help protect and disguise your intentions, as well as allow you to carry on some conversation without fear of an outside party comprehending (or caring) about the content and context of what is being said.

<u>**Activity 2:**</u>

Look at the following three pictures and write out either a SALUTE report or a SALT report, describing what you observe in each photograph. You will notice that the following images get progressively harder to decipher the number of people present, but the activity is quite clear. You can also choose other photographs from the Internet or take your own photos for future analysis to develop this skill further.

Photo courtesy of www.pixabay.com

Photo #1 – What do you observe?

____

____

____

____

____

____

____

____

____

____

____

____

____

____

Photo courtesy of www.pixabay.com

Photo #2 – What do you observe?

____
____
____
____
____
____
____
____
____
____
____
____
____
____
____

Photo courtesy of www.pixabay.com

Photo #3 – What do you observe?

____

____

____

____

____

____

____

____

____

____

____

____

____

____

Sources and Citations:

[1]https://forwardobserver.com/building-blocks-of-intelligence-salute-and-salt-reporting/

There are many limitations that affect one's ability to successfully implement Gray Man Tactics. Some of those limitations are related directly to some myths that need to be both acknowledged and debunked. Most people interested in the subject know what a Gray Man is. However, to understand the limitations, we must also acknowledge what the Gray Man is not with the following statements.

The Gray Man Is Not Prepping

This may come as a surprise because it is often discussed in preparedness and survival magazines. Someone using Gray Man tactics may be a prepper, but the skill set is not exclusive to prepping. The Gray Man principle is a skill set that can be learned and used prior to and during catastrophic events, however, it is not the act of being prepared or stocking up supplies in case of natural or man-made disasters.

Prepping, when implemented wisely and properly, eliminates or reduces the need to enter the public arena for supplies and services. The Gray Man principle is more focused on concealment in plain sight. Prepping, and keeping those preparation stockpiles safe from prying and curious eyes has more to do with the wise practices of OPSEC than the specific Gray Man skill set. Yes, the Gray Man skill set is an effective tool to have in your survival resources but understand that it does lose its effectiveness when the demands placed on the skill set exceed its designed intent. That intent is, of course, concealment within the urban environments.

In an emergency or crisis, any person out wandering around would be assumed to be looking for food/supplies or looking for trouble. So, entering the public arena automatically casts suspicion upon you. That suspicion would further be magnified if a curfew were in place and individuals choosing to violate that curfew would be subject to intense scrutiny and interrogation if apprehended.

The Gray Man Is Not Invisibility

The Gray Man is all about concealment. Typical camouflage apparel often will not work in an urban environment. People belong and are expected to be seen and present in an urban environment. The goal is to have anyone looking for you or having an active surveillance on you is to have them need more concrete identifiers to distinguish you from the other members of society present in the same area. Think of it in terms of a herd of zebras. Zebras, despite having a general appearance of black and white stripes, each zebra within the herd has unique stripes. But the required scrutiny and attention to detail to single out the one female zebra with 81 black stripes and 83 white stripes, starting with black from the neck at an 87 degree down angle left to right and having a solid white kneecap on the right rear leg would be much more time consuming to identify it amongst the other zebras within the herd.

Despite being physiologically the same, most people have significant identifying traits that others use to identify us. As such, we are not capable of completely masking our presence from anyone determined to find or identify us. The best we can do is obscure our most significant features and attempt to blend and match the appearance and mannerisms of others around us.

The Gray Man Is Not A Lone Wolf

Better stated, the Gray Man *should not* be a lone wolf. Yes, there will be times and situations where one may be physically alone. Depending on the environment, being alone without any type of back-up or overwatch acting as a second pair of eyes is extremely dangerous. Certain field operative work dictates working alone for the sake of pretexts and appearances. The lone wolf mentality is dangerous and puts you at a disadvantage if you find yourself in a predicament requiring assistance. Without having someone watching your back as an ally, it requires you to be even more vigilant to ensure your own safety.

The concept of having a partner or team is not as hindering as it is often portrayed in movies, with the clichéd macho attitude of, "I always work alone." There should not be a feeling of co-joined at the hip or smothering, but rather a balance of space and maintaining an eyes-on status. Oftentimes, this portrayal of reluctance is merely a vehicle to drive a narrative or plot twist involving betrayal or the existence of a mole attempting to thwart the group's objective.

Operating under the notion that only you are trustworthy sets you up for failure and incapable of taking on tasks that are beyond the ability of one person to accomplish.

The Gray Man Is Not Infallible

Because the execution of the Gray Man principles and tactics lies primarily within the realm of human behavior and the intentional modification of behavior for its success, eventually our "normal" behaviors cease to remain effectively hidden. Furthermore, because the application of Gray Man principles is subjective regarding our perception and interpretation of societal baselines, we can sometimes wrongly apply the principles at the wrong time, misunderstand the cultural context, or accidentally create unintended stimuli.

The Gray Man Is Not Sustainable

Just as the Gray Man principle is not infallible, it is neither sustainable. It cannot be subconsciously maintained. It does not have an active crypsis component allowing it to automatically sense, interpret, and match the surroundings. As such, the body can only "put on the act" for so long before it reverts to the habitual and subconscious. In addition, the mental fatigue of prolonged/sustained immersion into the act of engaging gray tactics, grows when activities are extended to interfere or hamper other physiological needs such as food and sleep.

As mentioned in my first *Gray Man* book, some of these are genetic and physiological which we have no or little control over. We cannot make ourselves taller or shorter, nor can we stop the aging process, no matter how desperate we are to retain our youthful vitality.

Fortunately, there are areas we can control and manipulate in our favor. It does not mean that they are 100 percent successful or come without a significant effort on our part. Nevertheless, these things can be changed in varying degrees. Because these limitations can hamper our ability to blend into an environment, I have developed and acronym to identify these potential limitations.

The HAMPERR Acronym

Habits
Appearance
Mannerisms
Patronage
Eye Contact
Repeat **R**ecognition

Habits – Everybody has habits, both good and bad. Most habits carry a negative connotation or stigma with them, but believe it or not, even good habits can create stimuli for someone else. For example, daily exercise is a good habit. It is highly recommended by doctors. But if you habitually schedule your training sessions at a certain time, a certain location, or certain days of the week, you create a pattern that can be noticed.

There is an old saying that goes, "When I do something good, no one remembers; but when I do something bad, no one forgets." Unfortunately, this is oftentimes true.   Think of someone you know. How many of their habits can you list? I know this exercise can be subjective and is skewed in terms of personal perception and idiosyncrasies, but I am willing to safely say you started with bad or negative habits first. These could go all the way back to when you first met this person or one that appeared shortly thereafter. You may have discovered it on your own or it was pointed out to you by someone else. These habits may not be deal breakers in terms of maintaining or beginning associations, but rather an acknowledgement that everyone has flaws, idiosyncrasies, and shortcomings.

Bad habits such as smoking or excessive drinking can create additional stimuli in the perception of others. People have tendencies to notice habits that are unpleasant or cast others in a poor light. Photo courtesy of www.pixabay.com.

Appearance – A lot of our personal clothing choices are a result of our own sense and definition of what style is. Our innate desire to "be somebody", admired, or respected can derail efforts to deploy Gray Man concepts effectively. Being labeled average is usually considered to be a deriding remark or an evaluation on someone's ability or competency to a particular task. However, for the Gray Man principle to succeed in the concealment aspects, practitioners must find the law of averages within the cultural and social baseline and match them.

Our clothing choices are not always dictated by our personal choices, but rather by terms of employment or company policy. Where individuals are given the opportunity to choose, the effort should be made to choose styles and colors that provoke little stimuli. Photo courtesy of www.pixabay.com.

Mannerisms – Everyone has their own personality quirks, ticks, and habitual fidgets. We have verbal crutches, go-to phrases, manner of greetings, etc. People raise eyebrows or one corner of their mouth first when they smirk. They flick their hair, bounce their leg, shake or tap their foot. If you watch anyone long enough, you will pick up on their nervous ticks and physiological coping mechanisms.

This information is so crucial that several books on body language have been written. I am no expert on body language, but my first formal introduction to it was in college during the Interviews and Interrogations course as part of my Criminal Justice studies. The psychological implications and justifications presented behind certain body behaviors was simply fascinating. The way some of the investigators were able to establish truth and guilt from a line of questioning and watching what the interviewed subjects did with their hands and facial expressions goes beyond what I had previously though possible. To say it is nearly an art form is not an exaggeration. With practice, you can identify many of the basic body language signals with relative ease and careful observation.

Mannerisms and facial expressions, as well as nervous fidgeting can thwart efforts to remain lost in the crowd. Photo courtesy of www.pixabay.com.

Patronage – We shop at grocery stores and shops that are convenient based on the proximity to our residence or the certain items they stock that we want. Humans are still social creatures, so it is not uncommon to develop a recognizable acquaintance with a regular cashier or shop owner. We also tend to support friends and their business enterprises, as well as those owned and operated by their spouses or children. We tend to have a particular barber or hair stylist. If you cannot think of a particular store or restaurant you frequent, let your significant other, your children, or a close friend choose a gift card for you on your birthday. They will usually pick a store where you often shop.

Being a frequent repeat customer may be beneficial in terms of quality, selection, and convenience, but has the potential of detracting from the implementation of gray man tactics. Photo courtesy of www.pixabay.com.

Eye Contact – In most modern societies and cultures, eye contact during the exchange of salutations and greetings is regarded as polite and appropriate behavior. However, there are cultures where it is considered impolite, even offensive to look someone directly in the eye as it implies accusatory body language or a certain level of wrongdoing on their part.[1] For example, in many Asian countries, avoiding eye contact is a show of respect. So, if you were to assert yourself through eye contact, you would be considered very rude, confrontational, or maybe even hostile towards the recipient.

Repeat Recognition – How many times have you recognized the same person whom you do not know at a different location? Sometimes it twenty minutes later or it could be several hours later. It is for this reason that surveillance teams switch out often or "drop a tail" to reduce the chance of being spotted or recognized by the person of interest (POI).

Eye contact can lead to repeat recognition and creates a place holder in our memories. It is often short and just enough to recall features to make anonymity harder to achieve. Photo courtesy of www.pixabay.com.

The Seven Deadly Sins of the Gray Man

Practitioners of the Gray Man principles are not immune from outside influences, inner bias, or cognitive dissonance. We must continually be mindful of what and who is shaping our world view and our response. There are seven things I have listed that greatly impact our ability to maintain a gray status or operate with a proper degree of situational sense.

Several of these "sins" were previously mentioned in *Situational Sense* as awareness saboteurs. Again, I am using the first seven letters in the alphabet to aid in remembering each one. Let us look at them below:

A – Ambivalence
B – Boredom
C – Complacency/Context
D – Distractions
E – Ego/Escalation
F – Failure to Fix Failures
G - Guessing

Ambivalence – We get bombarded with so much negativity and bad news from most media outlets that it sometimes seems easier to ignore it or pay no attention to it until such an event affects us personally and jolts us back into reality. It is so easy to turn off the television or scroll past some new political scandal or natural disaster that seems to happen miles away from where we are physically. This unfortunately can breed feelings of apathy to the point we find ourselves uncaring and failing to show the proper respect, regard, and empathy towards others who find themselves on the unfortunate side of a catastrophe.

Boredom – Adopting Gray Man principles into everyday life may sound like something out of a spy novel. The reality of it when it is correctly implemented is more boring than watching paint dry in the middle of the night. It is an important part of clandestine field and tradecraft, but without a suspenseful soundtrack and the latest Hollywood star portraying the role, it is rather boring. If you start trying to spice things up, you are missing the point.

Complacency/Context – Ambivalence and Boredom add up to Complacency very quickly. If we start letting our guard down because we are tuning out the dangers happening elsewhere, we lull ourselves into believing that it is only happening in those other places. Worse yet, if we let boredom sway us too much, we let our guard down to see if anything will happen.

Distractions – There are so many things competing for our attention that it is easy to become distracted by a whole myriad of things. Advertisements are a great example. Marketers use color psychology and base physiological needs and desires to attract our attention. It used to be when I was younger, billboards had a single image on them. Today, the newer digital billboards offer the key to grabbing someone's attention: movement. Movement is what causes us to focus on something that has appeared in our peripheral vision. Advertisements that have flashing lights, bold colors, and cyclic change intervals have high success rates of being noticed. Add celebrities, comfort food/beverages, and scantily clad models and you now have a perfect storm pulling your attention away.

Ego/Escalation – If there one "sin" that is more egregious than others, I would certainly point to ego and escalation. Each one of us has a certain level of ego that dictates or at least influences our decisions and behaviors. Our pride tends to defend and puff up our personal bias regarding our own abilities and knowledge while downplaying risk and limitations. Having the foresight to willfully choose to walk away from a potential conflict can divert a situation from a path that could and should be avoided. Call it professionalism and courtesy. There is no doubt there are people who neither desire professionalism nor courtesy based off their behavior and attitude. But, at the end of the day, if no threat or physical harm was made towards you or those in your care, you simply walk away. Swallowing one's pride may keep one from swallowing someone else's fist and their own teeth.

Failure to Fix Failures — Self-realization does little good if we ignore areas where we need improvement. While mistakes for people engaged regularly in high-conflict professions can have life-altering consequences, not all mistakes and failures are fatal. The sole purpose of training and acquiring/maintaining skills is to reduce failures or mitigate them down to survivable ones.

Guessing — We must try to know as much about every situation we may find ourselves, based upon the facts, evidence, and information we can gather at the time. Does it mean that we may be wrong? Absolutely. We may miss it by a meter or a mile. But guessing that stems from complete ignorance of potential threats is not acceptable.

Other Hinderances

Lack of Patience
Stoic Display (lack of emotion or emotional intelligence)
Time Management
Stress

There are a few more limitations, but those will be addressed later in a separate chapter, as they tend to enter the realm of shortcomings where adopting Gray Man principles will no longer be of significant benefit. You may be able to list some other hinderances not mentioned here.

PRACTICAL SKILL-SET:

In this chapter, I talked about the Seven Deadly Sins of the Gray Man. So, it only makes sense if we refer to the limitations of the Gray Man principles as sin, that we use a similar religious term to correct them: repentance. The literal translation of repentance means "to turn and walk away from sin." I am not telling you to confess to a pastor or priest, but rather make the willful decision to proactively disengage from activities and behaviors that hamper your ability to effectively blend into an urban environment.

One of the best ways to learn about human behavior is to simply watch people. Casually observe them when they eat, when they wait for the bus or train, when and how they conversate with others. The key is not to stare or pay more attention longer than what is necessary to gather some basic information. After all that, take a self-reflective look at yourself and honestly ask, Do I do the same thing, or do I do something similar? Do I do something completely different? For example, when most people sit and wait for an extended amount of time, they begin to fidget. They look at their fingers. They pick lint or fuzzes off their clothes. All sorts of random things. It is far easier to self-analyze our hang-ups and habits when we soften the blow by observing someone else doing it first.

Take the time to use some in-depth self-evaluation methods and objectively and truthfully put yourself under the proverbial microscope. Ask yourself the tough questions. Analyze your strengths and weaknesses. Confide in friends, family, and training partners to get feedback for areas of improvement and strategies and goals to flip those weaknesses into the strength's column.

You can list them below:

____

____

____

____

____

____

____

____

____

____

____

____

____

With the habits listed above, determine which ones have the potential of being detrimental to you or make the implementation of certain Gray Man tactics more difficult. Make the conscious effort to replace minor quirks, substitute nuisance habits for more constructive ones, and quit any bad habits that pose any type of short or long-term negative effects on your life.

Like anyone else, I too, have more than my fair share of personality flaws and habits that I both need and want to correct. So, do not think you are alone in this area. Be sure to seek out any professional help necessary for you to be successful in any lifestyle changes you make.

Back in the end of Chapter 7 where I discussed the limitations of the Gray Man, I alluded to other limitations in which the Gray Man principles no longer work to the degree necessary to be considered effective and lifesaving. As much as we would rather have a contingency plan that is universal and all-encompassing to address every survival and evasion scenario, the reality is that no such plan exists. When one plan does not work, another must be put into motion to adapt and overcome the dynamic changes placed before us.

Sensitization

Eventually, as the public becomes more aware of individuals seeking to remain concealed among the fringes of everyday society, they will become hyper-aware of people trying not to bring attention to themselves. This process is generally slow, but as more and more political and economic instability arises, further feeding an "us vs. them" mentality, it will be more recognizable. With world events as they are and their current course, it is highly unlikely that we would see a desensitizing trend anytime soon.

The more aware people start becoming and beginning to adopt and adapt the Gray Man principles, they will become more identifiable. This book, and its predecessor, are an unfortunate double-edged sword in this regard. To make the information available to those wanting it, I am disseminating information that some people would rather have suppressed or hidden. Their reason is so they may continue to walk freely while the rest of society continues in ignorance.

Part of this increase will also be directly correlated to the many novices unsuccessfully attempting to apply the principles without sufficient practice prior to the events precipitating its necessary implementation.   Certain events will force individuals to meet physiological needs for survival and in those attempts to obtain those supplies and fulfillments, individuals will likely compromise themselves through insufficient amounts of practice and prior planning.

Statutes

As soon as enough legislators and unelected bureaucrats begin taking notice of the potential freedom of movement created by implementing Gray Man tactics, they will begin their attempt to restrict certain types of clothing and accessories. This type of governmental tyranny has already been established and continually encroached upon with each new crime bill introduced. These bills are almost always a renewed attempt to subvert or remove what little we have of the Second Amendment.

Financial institutions have already started with their enforcement of policies prohibiting ball caps, sunglasses, helmets, and hooded sweatshirts in bank lobbies. Security guards at these institutions are likely acquainted with those attempting to commit robbery, and because many of the robbers wear such apparel, the law-abiding citizen bears the brunt of the policy.

As time goes by and more and more individuals take more proactive steps to disrupt a government's or institution's ability to identify people. Law and policy makers propose changes to curtail those attempts. Photo courtesy of www.pixabay.com

Suspension

Suspension seems almost the gray area between Statutes and Stratocracy. It may be heavily reliant upon statutes and policies to convince law-abiding citizens to remain in the "law-abiding" column. Social pressure and norms may be used to shame and alienate those individuals who will not conform to socially acceptable choices or the choices presented by government or institutions. One need not look beyond the current "Cancel Culture" in our society as evidence to the described modus operandi.

As I stated earlier, because of the non-committal and widely accepted neutrality of gray from a stimuli point of view, both frightened people and people in authority are looking for definitive, black or white decisions from you. Anything varying from those two choices may result in confusion, animosity, or provocation on the part of others.

In this situation, the police are looking for black or white/right or wrong/yes or no/ compliant or non-compliant behavior. Photo courtesy of www.pixabay.com

Stratocracy

Stratocracy is the technical term for a military-led form of government. In other words, martial law. When governmental authorities begin enforcing checkpoints and curfews, the Gray Man tactics become increasingly more difficult to use. If you are seen out past the designated curfew, you will get stopped. With fewer people on the streets for fear of whatever penalties are deemed prudent to deter violators, your ability to move unnoticed through a crowd becomes a moot point.

PRACTICAL SKILL-SET:

Using the space provided below and the previous information you have read, think about the steps you might take to overcome some of the circumstances mentioned in this chapter.

What would you do or how could you circumvent a situation where more and more people are now trying to implement and deploy the same tactics to go about unnoticed or noticed less frequently?

____

____

____

____

____

____

____

What would you do or how could you circumvent a situation where the government or a private business/institution has recently changed a policy or a statute prohibiting certain apparel or demanding the use of other apparel (i.e., masks) for health and safety reasons?

____

____

____

____

____

____

____

What would you do or how could you circumvent a situation where there is a temporary suspension of certain rights through a declaration of martial law in order to go about your business?

____

____

____

____

____

____

____

What would you do or how could you circumvent a situation where a military-run government or newly installed government contrary to the guidelines found within the Constitution to go about your business and providing for yourself and family?

____

____

____

____

____

____

____

The chaos is coming. In some cities and states, it has already arrived and gaining strength with a growing potential for greater destruction. Just like tornadoes and hurricanes, they will leave behind pathways littered with debris and shattered dreams, and broken lives.

What is a TROUBLE Kit?

Having served in the military, my affinity for acronyms seems second nature. The evidence is literally scattered throughout this book and its predecessors. While other veterans dislike them, they do have value and serve as helpful reminders to recall information. The acronym I have coined for the TROUBLE Kit stands for:

Terrorism
Riots/Rebellions

Occupations
Unrest
Blockades
Lawlessness/Looting
Engage/Evade/Escape

A TROUBLE Kit is a hybrid blend of Bug-Out Bag, Get-Home Bag, heavy-duty SERE kit, Vehicle Emergency kit and EDC kit. It focuses heavily on utilizing Gray Man principles to remove yourself from a non-permissive environment or an area that has degraded into an unsafe level of social chaos with no active rule of law or legitimate enforcement oversight. It incorporates the use of specific tools that handle certain tasks beyond the capabilities of your EDC. Keep in mind that there is the potential for your TROUBLE Kit to get you into just that: Trouble. While the tools of your kit may be legal to own, contextually and the totality of the contents may paint a wrong conclusion in the eyes of law enforcement.

Protests can quickly escalate to rioting, looting, and destruction of public and private property. Photo courtesy of www.pixabay.com

Deploying your TROUBLE Kit

When you consider yourself to be in an extremely dangerous environment where the likelihood of sustaining injury is high, it is time to deploy your TROUBLE kit. You may find yourself in a position where you must travel through parts of a city where law enforcement has been overwhelmed, overrun, or ordered to stand down and retreat.

While the windows may be boarded up to prevent damage to windows and unauthorized entry, they can be a potential fire hazard when someone armed with a Molotov Cocktail shows up. Photo courtesy of www.pixabay.com

What should you have in a TROUBLE Kit?

Specific kit content will depend greatly on the environmental conditions from which you are trying to extract yourself. In addition to the tools and supplies listed, acquiring the training for the effective use of such tools is fundamentally necessary. While most of these tools are not illegal to own, how you utilize them within a TROUBLE scenario may cross the lines of legality. At this point, however, legality is no longer a consideration over the necessity for removing yourself from a non-permissive, hostile environment. For example, a direct escape route may not be available, so you may have to hole up in a building. Using door wedges or a chain to secure a fire door to prevent its opening has now crossed that line of legality.

TROUBLE kit contents are grouped together with a simple ABC acronym, based upon their function and purpose. A functional kit should include: ACCESS/DENIAL TOOLS, BASELINE, CASUALTIES and CONTINGENCIES. As I did not mention it earlier, now is the perfect time to interject a necessary requirement concerning your TROUBLE kit. Your kit must be portable and lightweight as possible.

ACCESS/DENIAL TOOLS

Many of the tools within the TROUBLE Kit, when carried together, are more likely to resemble a burglar's bag of tools, so it is important to not only carry the kit discreetly, but only carry it when necessary. However, under some circumstances, the practicality of obeying the law would unreasonably expect you to sacrifice your safety for the sake of complying with certain laws. So, in that regard, you will incur considerable risk of potential arrest and/or prosecution if you find no option other than to trespass onto private property to escape or leave an area. Some common tools to obtain for your kit could be:

- Lock-pick set
- Automatic center punch or another glassing breaking device
- Small bolt cutters
- Wire cutters
- Small wrecking bar or prybar

- Small screwdriver set (with select security/tamper resistant bits)
- 6mm shackle diameter (or larger) padlock
- A length of medium to heavy duty chain
- Door wedges
- Rubber bands
- Tape
- Heavy duty cable ties or 4" diameter (or larger) hose clamps

Lock pick sets assist in entering locked areas and buildings. It is important to remember that breaking and entering is still a criminal offense and poses serious legal implications. Photo courtesy of www.pixabay.com

Lock-Pick Set

A lock-pick set is an essential piece of Gray Man gear. During an escape and evasion event, it may be necessary to gain access to buildings or areas which are locked. Lock-pick sets require an extensive amount of practice to be both quick and proficient. Fortunately, you can find lock-pick sets online and many of the SERE and survival training providers have recommended kits and retailers from whom they get their course supplies. I cannot emphasize enough the importance of practicing with a lock-pick set. This skill requires quite a bit of finesse to quickly manipulate locks. Most homes have many styles of locks throughout, providing plenty of free practice. It never is as easy or as fast as it is portrayed in all the spy movies.

Automatic Center Punch

One of my personal favorite tools is an automatic center punch. The hardened tip works well for scratching or etching, as well as breaking glass. It also functions as an emergency self-defense tool. The pointed end is hard enough to plunge into soft tissue areas. Most automatic center punches are made from brass, so the blunt end can be used as a kubotan-type striking weapon. They are also inexpensive and easy to replace without anyone ever questioning the purchase.

Another option is the small Res-Q-Me tool. It houses both a glass break tool and protected razor blade for cutting seat belt straps. The razor can also cut plastic wire ties and rope with diameters less than 8mm.

The Res-Q-Me vehicle escape tool. Photo courtesy of https:// www.eliteoutdoorgear.com.au/?post_type=product&p=4536

Bolt Cutters

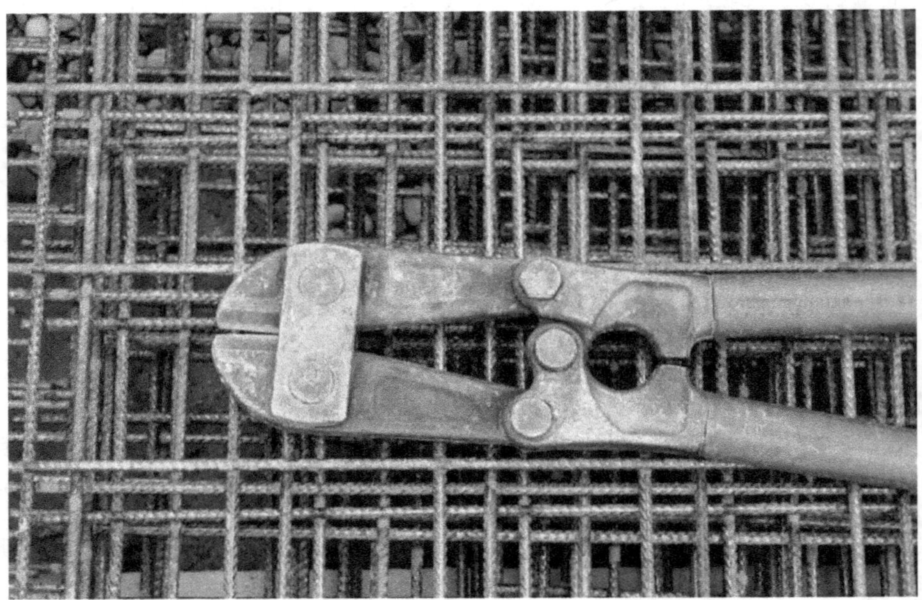

Bolt cutters are often necessary for removing chains and padlocks in the event the lock cannot be picked. When possible, cut the lock or cut a chain link that allows for the reuse of the maximum length of chain. Photo courtesy of www.pixabay.com

The most effective and efficient bolt cutters are too cumbersome to carry in a TROUBLE kit, adding significant weight to your bag. However, there are smaller versions that will fit inside a bag and still handle chain links and low security locks of 6mm or less. Obviously, the closer to the 6mm chain diameter, the more likely the cutters will struggle or require multiple attempts to cut through the material. High security and hardened steel locks are difficult to cut, so it is better to try to cut the chain, rather than the lock. Sometimes the next tool listed here fares better in creating an access point.

Wrecking Bar or Pry Bar

The wrecking bar is often called the burglar's best friend. It works well as a mechanical lever to separate doors and windows from their respective frames. It can break glass with ease and effectively becomes a club to either persuade compliance or deter attack. Carrying this tool, much like the bolt cutters, creates an air of suspicion, so it is necessary to carry one small enough to fit inside a bag yet large enough to provide the necessary leverage for access. You want to avoid carrying the item in your hand until you need to use it, as the stimuli you create will most certainly attract unwanted attention.

A wrecking bar is a common tool used by burglars and thieves to bypass residential doors and windows. Photo courtesy of www.pixabay.com

Screwdriver Set with Security Bits

Your TROUBLE kit should undoubtedly contain a screwdriver set. Here again, screwdrivers are a common improvised weapon that most people give little attention to, as they are so commonplace. You are more likely to get quizzical looks for the security bits rather than the screwdriver itself. However, it is unlikely that you will be showing the contents of your TROUBLE kit to anyone.

A compact screwdriver with interchangeable hex drive bits is a wise addition to your TROUBLE kit. Along with added security bits, you will have better access to alarm and electronics panels. Photo courtesy of www.pixabay.com

Padlock and Chain

Having a spare padlock and chain in your TROUBLE kit is a good idea for a few reasons. First, it allows you to resecure an area you have entered in the event you needed to cut an existing lock or the chain. As you will no doubt have the key to open this lock, you save time by not having to repick the lock or risk leaving the area unsecured. Second, the padlock on the end of a chain may be used an improvised defensive tool. Its metal construction and significant weight is a formidable weapon should the need arise. Depending on the length of chain, it can keep a knife attacker at bay and maybe convince him to find easier prey. One thing I recommend is cutting a length of old bicycle tire tubing and slide the chain through it. This protects other items within your TROUBLE kit and helps deaden the characteristic clinking sound of the links rubbing and banging together.

Carrying a padlock and a length of chain allows you to resecure an access point to prevent others from entering after you. It also gives the illusion that no one has accessed the area. Photo courtesy of www.pixabay.com

Rubber Bands and Tape

If you have ever seen demonstrations or videos of how to circumvent sliding chain locks, you will understand the necessity for carrying rubber bands and tape in your TROUBLE kit. If you absolutely need to gain access through a locked door, you want to minimize the damage to the structural integrity of that door. It allows you to re-use and benefit from the security the door provides.

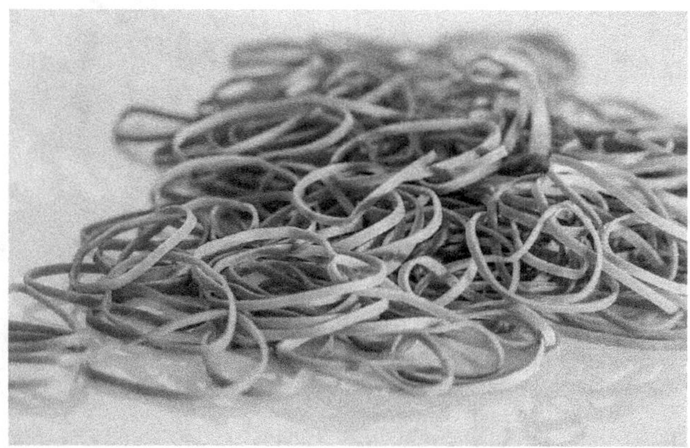

Carrying half a dozen rubber bands and a small roll of electrical or duct tape can aid it defeating sliding chain locks. Photo courtesy of www.pixabay.com

Cable Ties

Cable ties are essential if you need to temporarily restrain someone to facilitate an escape from an unlawful detention. However, this method is, at best temporary, as captors are well-versed in the same SERE methods you have employed to aid in your escape. It is extremely important to remember, in most countries, detaining someone unlawfully is a serious offense, in which you had better have a justifiable reason for doing so if the situation makes its way into the court system. Even then, there is no guarantee that you will be able to avoid criminal prosecution despite any self-defense or fear for your safety argument you provide.

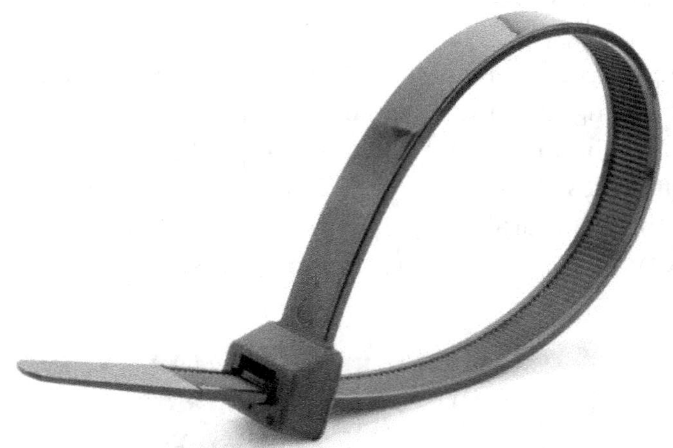

Black heavy-duty cable ties can be used to temporarily secure several things, including people, if necessary. Photo credit: https://www.securecableties.com/ extra-heavy-duty-175-250-lbs10

They can also be used to delay entry into a location when other locking methods are not available. You can also resecure portions of chain link fencing with strategically placed cable ties. Try to avoid bright colored cable ties, as they are easily discovered. Gray or black colored cable ties work best, with black ties having far better resistance to UV rays and are better suited for outdoor applications.

For a stronger, longer-lasting solution, you may want to consider the use of large hose clamps. These still carry the same warnings if used for purposes other than their intended purpose, however, their advantages in improvised situations could prove invaluable. When used as an improvised restraining device, they are better suited than cable ties and traditional handcuffs.

First, the clamps are made from stainless steel, which makes them harder to cut and will produce significantly more pain and discomfort throughout an escape attempt. Second, they require more manual dexterity to defeat. Third, it requires a tool that is much more difficult to conceal on your person. A flat head screwdriver will turn the screw, but the most effective tool is the ¼ inch socket. Fourth, most SERE courses focus on handcuff manipulation and cable tie escape. So, in the event your adversary has had formal SERE counter-custody training, you may throw a monkey wrench into their escape efforts.

The amount of manual dexterity and tools required to release and loosen hose clamps make them a better improvised detention device. Photo credit: https://www.ebay.com/ itm/Large-Stainless-Steel-Hose-Band-Clamps-5-4-3-inch-48-127mm-1-7-8-5-0-B3-/332746248697

BASELINE

Baseline is critical in all camouflage and concealment endeavors. As scenarios of civil unrest and riots often play out in urban environments, utilizing Gray Man principles to blend in is key. Adapting clothing choices and behaviors that mirror your immediate surroundings is of utmost importance. The clothing recommendations in your TROUBLE Kit should resemble the common apparel of rioters and protestors, with a heavy concentration on covering the face and hands. Even before the COVID-19 pandemic, rioters and protestors in the past covered their faces to hide their identities. As both the hype and reality of COVID-19 continues, the use of a facemask or bandanna is a gift to walk around with a certain level of anonymity. For you, this creates an opportunity to match their baseline if you cannot access your vehicle or other method of faster transportation.

These individuals are not identifiable due to the face coverings and sunglasses. Some of the facial technology available today still has difficulty identifying individuals purposely covering features the software uses to measure spacing and symmetry to match individuals within police databases. Photo courtesy of www.pixabay.com

As we have seen through the various news outlets, there are some common clothing themes. Black Lives Matter and Antifa protestors are often wearing black or other dark colored clothing. This is the only time I would recommend wearing black clothes as a form of camouflage, as it allows you to conceal yourself and move within their ranks with hopefully less contact and conflict. It serves as an unofficial uniform and identifies/unites them. Consider pretexting your behavior as that of an active participant by repeating similar chants and slogans. While it may turn your stomach to shout profanities or phrases that are in opposition to your patriotism or personal ideologies, it may be necessary to blend in enough so you can move unhassled until you can find an exit point.

- Bandanna, facemask, or neck gaiter
- Dark colored ball cap or beanie
- Dark colored hooded sweatshirt
- Non-descript/non-tactical sling bag or backpack

Safety pinning an activism campaign or recognized logo of a movement or group shows or pretends to show allegiance or alignment with the principles promoted within that movement or group. Photo courtesy of www.pixabay.com

While a large majority of rioters and protestors show up empty handed or with typical handwritten placards, this is a trend that is going to change. There have already been photographed instances of people using baseball bats as the handle for homemade signs. As these groups become more brazen and hostile, the items they carry into this battlefield will morph into improvised weapons, along with the means to carry them hands-free until needed. Backpacks provide that mobility as well as keeping contraband and weapons out of sight. Therefore, a backpack is the best option for carrying your TROUBLE Kit items. Having an assortment of patches, pins, or ribbons in support of a particular movement to safety pin or tie to the backpack may add to the pretext, but it may provoke others within the mob should you mistakenly "support" a clashing viewpoint.

CASUALTY/CONTINGENCIES

With any breakdown of civility and order, the potential of injury and victimhood escalates exponentially. Some of those sustained injuries may be indirectly or unintentionally caused. A group, panicked and terrified, violently pushes past you to escape and pushes through a window or your finger(s) get wedged in a door. It happens. While not deliberately targeted, you now have injuries requiring some basic first aid. Other injuries may require a more extensive trauma kit to address larger or more critical wounds. To treat a wide range of injuries, I recommend carrying a full trauma kit to treat gunshots, lacerations, or other types of injuries resulting in major blood loss.

Another item that may prove useful is Johnson's baby shampoo. A 2018 study published by the Western Journal of Emergency Medicine discussed the ineffectiveness of these items to reduce the pain and duration caused by OC and CS contamination. Despite this, it is often recommended to assist in flushing and removing residue, as both chemical agents are oil-based and tend to stay on the skin longer. If nothing else, it can be used to barter for passage.[1] Below is a list of other potentially useful items for your TROUBLE kit.

- Trauma/First-aid kit
- Nitrile palmed, cut-resistant gloves
- Tinted goggles and/or eye protection
- Johnson's baby shampoo
- Dawn dish soap
- Hand sanitizer
- 1.5 – 2-liter bottle of water

As rioters and protestors educate themselves more regarding specific equipment to minimize the effects of crowd control and riot dispersal agents, the inclusion of a full-fledged gas mask may be necessary to blend in better. However, a situation may arise where the gas mask may be considered an item of value, especially if someone releases tear gas cannisters or other noxious substances via aerial dispersion.

The author assumes the reader would already be carrying other tools such as a concealed firearm, a knife, a flashlight, and a SERE kit as part of an EDC kit.

OPTIONAL "PROTESTOR" GEAR

Part of what defines protestors is their ability to make noise, attempting to make their voices heard. You may have seen protestors banging away on a cowbell for both its general irritation and its ability to establish chant cadence. Swapping out a hardwood drumstick (typically hickory) with an aluminum alloy drumstick provides with an improvised baton as a defensive weapon. The cowbell serves as an expedient door lock for outward-opening entry/exit doors, as it easily slides over the top hinge. Granted, it is not as secure and heavy duty as those commercially designed for school and office active shooter lockdowns. Here again, it is about pretexting and carrying items that fit the contextual environment.

Another item I have packed in my TROUBLE Kit is a small travel size can of Lynx Deodorant/body spray. It smells horrible in my opinion and only takes a small amount of the product to overpower a small area quickly. The premise behind its carry serves a couple of purposes.

First, as the product is popular among today's younger generations for its ability to mask unwanted odors, if you end up smelling a bit like them, they may be more accepting of your presence. Second, you can use the spray to mark people and using it as a *last resort* defensive spray aimed at the eyes, nose, and mouth. Third, it serves as a makeshift incendiary device or mini flamethrower with the aid of a cigarette lighter from the EDC. This is highly dangerous and illegal, but I list it as an option when no other course of action for self-protection is available.

Sources and Citations:

[1]https://www.ncbi.nlm.nih.gov/pmc/articles/PMC5851502/

The need for stealthier supplies becomes more important when dealing with sanctions or non-permissive environments (NPEs). Therefore, in this chapter, we are looking first at tools and accessories that are less detectable with scanners and sensors. When the intention to carry an item is to defeat modern weapon detection technology, one must understand the limited selection and composition of the tool itself. This often means anything made of metal is not going to pass the concealability test.

As much as I would like to disclose what some of these items are and how to conceal them, prudence dictates that I practice good OPSEC for the sake of needing to use these items in the future. However, Internet search engines (I recommend DuckDuckGo) will still provide knowledge on some basic items, but if you are going to spend a great deal of time within well-known and documented NPEs, you should seek out professional training if you have not acquired it already.

Scanners, Sensors, and Searches

The most common electronic detection devices are those found in airport security checkpoints, courtrooms, and schools. Their purpose is to indicate with lights or audible tones when metal objects pass through the electromagnetic field generated by the two poles. X-Ray machines are also used to look through bags to detect objects hidden within other innocent-looking items.

It is important to realize that the likelihood of defeating these types of detection methods is very slim. There are items that can slip through sensors and the casual glance during periods of low threat levels, but it is necessary to understand that attempting to knowingly bring prohibited or contraband items into a controlled area is illegal. No amount of justification will make it otherwise.

You may be presented with a situation where police or some other entity (legitimate or otherwise) decides it necessary to conduct physical searches of anyone entering an area. Hopefully, you would have had the good sense to recognize the check point prior so it could be avoided. Constitutional rights may be suspended or ignored in the eyes of some, despite the government's responsibility to prevent those rights concerning searches and seizures from being infringed.

Sidearms

It should go without saying that if you have the legal means to do so, any weapon you carry on your person should be done in a concealed manner. I am a strong opponent against open carry, even in jurisdictions where it is lawful, commonplace, and socially acceptable to do so. The firearm, by its inherent capabilities, produces strong opinions and feelings which in return creates excess stimuli resulting in apprehension, anxiety, and even outright panic in some people. Therefore, it is imperative when considering Gray Man principles that every effort to keep weapons, especially firearms, out of view of the public.

Concealed carry firearms should be small enough to conceal without "printing" through clothing, yet of an appropriate caliber to provide both ballistic stopping power and capacity. Photo courtesy of www.pixabay.com

I now live in Australia where it is illegal to carry any concealed firearm. This is a drastic departure from what was permissible when I lived in the United States. Any justification that may exist has an incredibly difficult licensing process to obtain certain types of firearms. Despite my ideological opposition to the legislative reasoning in Australia, I am still obligated to abide by the rules. Firearm ownership is legal here with strict guidelines and licensing procedures. One must have a "genuine reason" for ownership and self-defense is not an acceptable qualifier in that regard. It is one less defense tool available to me, but I make sure to have other legal and improvised tools available to me.

A big part of mindset of self-defense relies on your ability and desire to avoid situations in the first place. An ounce of prevention is worth more than a pound of cure. Anyone strapped and armed to the teeth are going to get looks, so the less conspicuous you can present yourself, the better.

However, when it comes to carrying items that are either prohibited by law or likely to be confiscated in compliance with condition of entry policies, it becomes a bit harder to conceal some items. That is not to say it cannot be done from a practical standpoint, as I am a firm believer in "where there's a will, there's a way."

Please note that this is not a recommendation or permission to violate the law. I am not an attorney. You, and only you, must face the consequences of your actions should you engage in this type of behavior. With that said, do I believe it to be necessary to violate the law to protect yourself? Absolutely yes! The reason for this is simple. There is no smartphone app, that when used, makes a police officer magically appear like a genie out of your phone. Nor does a bodyguard, prosecutor, or judge appear at your side to frighten an attacker away. Police response times are notoriously infamous for being slow. With most violent encounters lasting under a minute, no matter how you try to pin the responsibility of safety and personal protection onto police, they and the courts have already freed police from any liability. That means your safety will always revert to you.

All the good-intentioned lawmakers view society as a collective, even though it takes *individuals* to establish that collective. They will ignore individual rights to protect society by reducing the quantity and availability of items rather than promote individual rights. Politicians and policy makers incorrectly and inaccurately claim the increased quantity and availability of weapons results in higher crime rates. Crime statistics have nearly debunked this logic to the point of insanity. Weapons in the hands of responsible, self-protected citizens reduces crime against both individuals and the rest of society. Poorly allocated and misspent tax dollars do not effectively protect you through the hiring of more police. You are still your own best defense. Get skills and use them, if and when necessary.

Stealth Safes

This water bottle diversion safe has ample space for a SERE kit or mini survival kit. The primary concerns are to prevent accidental opening and keep the weight of the added contents from reducing the safe's efficiency if casually inspected. Photo by author.

A stealth safe, also known as a diversion safe, is a tangible object that has the *benign* appearance and feel of a legitimate, intended purpose item. Most diversion safes are used in homes to hide small sized valuables out of sight from opportunistic burglars who want to make quick searches and discoveries. Due to the potential risk of detection by human and electronic means, burglars tend to be rather quick in their searches to avoid witnesses and arrival of the police should an alarm sound alerting the owners and/or monitoring service of the intrusion.

Water bottle diversion safes (and diversion safes, in general) are often overlooked. Use the complacency of others to carry items requiring discreet means. Photo by author.

There are also more personally invasive safes, such as the infamous "prison safe" which consists of a smooth, hollow plastic or metal container which is inserted into the rectum. For obvious sanitation and hygiene reasons, this method is not recommended. But under dire circumstances, it may have to be considered and utilized. I mention merely for the sake of being comprehensive.

Old-fashioned money belts, as well as some of the modern-day equivalents have multiple storage areas hidden within the belt material to place escape tools, currency, and other items on your person. Here again, the less tactical the belt looks, the less likely it will be assumed to contain EDC supplies or valuables.

Scrapping

Scrapping is the same thing as intentionally discarding or dumping items to escape from someone who wants a particular thing in your possession. Typically, this is a wallet or jewelry, but it can be anything the perpetrator deems valuable to them.

This fake vehicle key fob is a non-working decoy that can serve as a diversion safe or a dump key, similar in principle to a dump wallet. The key can be tossed as a distraction while you make your escape or deploy defensive countermeasures.[2]

As fake key fobs are designed to come apart to serve as a mini cache, it is a good idea to super-glue the pieces together if you are planning to use the fob solely as a dump key. The reason is when you toss the fob away, the ground impact may cause the fob to break apart, rendering its deceptive abilities moot.

RFID sleeves are good idea for your actual credit and debit cards or other cards that may contain your personal information. Do not limit their use to just vacation and foreign travel. The sleeves are inexpensive enough to give your dump wallet a more believable and authentic look, if your "protecting" a bunch of bogus cards. Photo by author.

Plastic gift cards can take an edge like a knife blade. It is not as sharp or effective as a steel blade, but it can serve as a last-ditch tool to slice an attacker's face. The microscopically jagged edge will certainly have a good chance of retaining the attacker's DNA. When carried in RFID sleeves, the edge is not visible. In most cases, authorities are not permitted to visually inspect individual credit cards stored inside a wallet. Metal cards will obviously set off sensors, so a plastic alternative is better suited for use within NPEs. Plastic credit and debit cards logically belong in a wallet, so if the sensors do not indicate a foreign object, the prevailing notion is the wallet contains only legitimate cards.

Sources and Citations:

https://www.itstactical.com/warcom/firearms/non-permissive-concealed-carry-tips/

[2]https://www.ebay.com.au/itm/2Pcs-Amazing-Stash-Car-Key-Safe-Compartment-Container-Safe-Secret-Hollow-Z/373190106510?_trkparms=aid%3D1110012%26algo%3DSPLICE.SOIPOST%26ao%3D1%26asc%3D20200420083544%26meid%3D3beba2410e184cbbbfd7404cc6b8b87b%26pid%3D100008%26rk%3D6%26rkt%3D12%26sd%3D37316 8458161%26itm%3D373190106510%26pmt%3D1%26noa%3D0%26pg%3D2047675%26algv%3DPromotedSellersOtherItemsV2%26brand%3DUnbranded&_trksid=p2047675.c100008.m2219

In the third quarter of 2020, several businesses and individuals who specialize in Gray Man tactics and products came together to form a loose cooperative on Instagram in an effort to reach a greater audience regarding Gray Man skills. As a result, I reached out to the group asking for scenario submissions. Those who were willing and able to provide a scenario for this book are individually credited for their submission and their business information can be found in the Training Resources section in the back of the book. Some contributors wished to remain anonymous for OPSEC reasons to which I was happy to oblige their requests

The individuals providing the scenarios are among some of the best in the business and are highly knowledgeable and have significant experience in the implementation of Gray Man tactics.

Scenario #1   *Author Contribution*

You have just finished filing your passport renewal at the downtown post office in your city. As you are leaving, you overhear employees discussing breaking news of a shooting that just occurred less than a mile away within the downtown district. The media has already reported the shooting as race-related or identified the race of both shooter and victim. Rioting has already begun due to the ongoing and increasing tensions with police and is escalating faster than riots in the past. Parking was at a premium and you were forced to use a multi-level parking complex several blocks away from your destination.

You arrive at your vehicle, only to find workers from the surrounding business are now desperately scrambling to leave and get home before the situation worsens, clogging the exit of the parking complex. Police, fire, and rescue units are being mobilized to the area and access in and out is being barricaded to contain the unrest. You phone a friend who lives nearby and arrange an extraction far away from the riot zone. However, to get to the extraction site, you must navigate through a hostile and potentially violent area. Public transport has now been halted for public safety concerns. One of the suggested travel routes requires you to pass within 100 yards of the police precinct where the involved officer is stationed.

You decide to leave your vehicle in the complex, as you can see those leaving the parking facility are having bottles and other objects thrown at their vehicles. Rioters are organizing human barricades and piling debris to obstruct traffic. You grab a prepared backpack from the trunk of your vehicle and head toward the furthest stairwell. You have little battery life on your phone and the cellular service is notoriously weak in the area.

On a scale ranging from 1 to 10, with 1 being the lowest and 10 being the highest, how much danger do you perceive yourself to be in?

1   2   3   4   5   6   7   8   9   10
Low   High

Write down the actions you would take:

____

____

____

____

____

____

____

____

____

What are some of the potential benefits from those actions taken?

____

____

____

____

____

____

____

____

____

What are some of the negative consequences?

____

____

____

____

____

____

____

____

What other factors would you take into consideration?

____

____

____

____

____

____

____

____

Scenario #2   ***Guest Contributor: Anonymous***

You and your spouse are on an interstate vacation and are shopping at a large mall complex. It is terribly busy and very crowded. Both of you have dressed conservatively in the hopes of keeping a low profile to avoid looking like out-of-towners. You are carrying concealed and have a small daypack with some EDC items too bulky to carry on your person. It is nearing 11:30am, with many patrons coming in for lunch or to do some quick shopping during their lunch break.

Your spouse decides to look inside a boutique store that is of no interest to you, so you mention that you will wait in the food court area nearby. While sitting, you watch people as they go about their business. Out of the corner of your eye, you see a man carrying a similar backpack and dressed so similarly to you that you decide to observe him further. He appears to casually look around as he makes his way to restrooms. The man comes out a few minutes later dressed in different clothes and without the backpack. He pulls out a cell phone while he walks by within earshot. You overhear him speaking excitedly/panicked in a foreign language. You are not certain of the exact language. It sounds distinctly Middle Eastern based on vocal inflections, and the only word you can mentally translate is "Allah".

You recall a recent news report regarding a tense and highly controversial peace agreement being brokered in the Middle East. In the area where the shopping mall is situated, there is a noticeable Jewish and Middle Eastern demographic, evidenced by some specialty stores featuring both Kosher and Halal approved food. The Department of Homeland Security and FBI websites have not updated national threat levels.

On a scale ranging from 1 to 10, with 1 being the lowest and 10 being the highest, how much danger do you perceive yourself to be in?

1   2   3   4   5   6   7   8   9   10
Low   High

Write down the steps you would take:

____

____

____

____

____

____

____

____

____

____

What are some of the potential benefits from those actions taken?

____

____

____

____

____

____

____

____

____

What are some of the negative consequences?

____

____

____

____

____

____

____

____

What other factors would you take into consideration?

____

____

____

____

____

____

____

____

____

____

Scenario #3   ***Guest Contributor: Anonymous***

Political unrest has begun across the nation after the result of a highly contested national election. Supporters of the winning party have openly called for the "punishment" of those supported and voted for the losing party. Violence has broken out in the larger cities, as well-organized and peaceful, yet vocal protests within the national Capitol complex and surrounding areas. There reports of some supporters viciously assaulted with some deaths occurring because of the attacks.

You find yourself on the losing side and now must go about your daily life avoiding the mayhem and minimizing or reducing any potential conflict with citizens and violent extremists looking to engage in acts likened to witch hunts and Gestapo-type gathering of "the enemy". Social media platforms have targeted supporters of the losing party and have begun suppressing and censoring comments and posts, while Big Tech companies have pulled the plug from host servers used by targeted groups to quash dissention, stop organization efforts, and prevent feared retaliation/insurrection towards the newly installed party in power.

You live in a relatively quiet suburb outside a major city that earlier in the year experienced massive riots and looting. The political demographic in the area is a straight 50/50 split with only a 1-2 percent fluctuation determining local and state governance. You have a casual, amiable relationship with many of your neighbors living on the same street. You have always been mindful of who puts out political candidacy support and yard signs, but now some of those neighbors have brazenly suggested identifying the "opposition" for targeted harassment and intimidation.

On a scale ranging from 1 to 10, with 1 being the lowest and 10 being the highest, how much danger do you perceive yourself to be in?

1   2   3   4   5   6   7   8   9   10
Low   High

Write down the steps you would take:

____
____
____
____
____
____
____
____
____

What are some of the potential benefits from those actions taken?

____
____
____
____
____
____
____
____
____

What are some of the negative consequences?

____

____

____

____

____

____

____

____

What other factors would you take into consideration?

____

____

____

____

____

____

____

____

____

Scenario #4   ***Guest Contributor: Wesley Superesse***

While traveling on vacation to Japan, you have a scheduled layover in Manila, Philippines. Unfortunately, you learn today is the first day of a planned strike by the Philippine National Police (PNP) due to the government putting a funding freeze in place, leaving PNP officers without pay for two months. Shortly after landing, a general announcement is made notifying travellers that all connecting flights are cancelled because of the protests and you are given a voucher for a three-night stay at a hotel across town. You have heard the Philippines has some great attractions, but you also know the Manila crime rate has been historically high.   With protests forming around the airport, you speculate an increase in criminal activity as you walk outside the arrival terminal to await a taxi.

The streets are busy, and you tightly hold your bag as passersby bump into you in the impending chaos mixed with the typical pedestrian congestion. You look and feel out of place wearing khaki pants and a button up shirt. You notice a lot of eyes on you while waiting for a taxi. Ten minutes go by and still no taxis. Locating the hotel using a map app on your phone, you learn it is a long three miles away through the city. You decide to set out on foot in the direction towards the hotel.

After 20 minutes of walking, you stop by a street vendor to purchase a bottle of water, only to discover that your travel wallet is missing. Your heart sinks as you realize all your cash, credit cards, and your passport are now gone, most likely in the hands of a pickpocket. The vendor kindly gives you the water and warns you to get off the streets. He tells you of the chatter about police buildings being targeted and one district station currently ablaze, as criminals and political activists have seized on the opportunity to destroy business and property because of the police strike. Where do you decide to go? The hotel, the US Embassy/Consulate building, or a police station?

On a scale ranging from 1 to 10, with 1 being the lowest and 10 being the highest, how much danger do you perceive yourself to be in?

1   2   3   4   5   6   7   8   9   10
Low   High

Write down the steps you would take:

____

____

____

____

____

____

____

____

____

____

What are some of the potential benefits from those actions taken?

____

____

____

____

____

____

____

____

____

____

What are some of the negative consequences?

____

____

____

____

____

____

____

____

What other factors would you take into consideration?

____

____

____

____

____

____

____

____

____

Appendices

The appendix section contains several infographics that have appeared on a few of my social media accounts and are relevant to both the Gray Man and Situational Sense topics. Full color digital versions are available for purchase through a third-party link on the Hidden Success Tactical website, www.hiddensuccesstactical.com.

10 COMMANDMENTS OF GRAY MAN
TACTICS and MINDSET
1. Do not create excess stimuli for others.
2. Be aware of others and your surroundings.
3. Maintain calmness and self-control.
4. Do not wear tactical clothing or gear.
5. Avoid bright-colored clothing/accessories.
6. Practice good OPSEC and PERSEC protocols.
7. Do not seek out conflicts.
8. Choose flight over fight when possible.
9. Learn and use counter-surveillance tactics.
10. Your safety is YOUR responsibility.
SENSES
SIGHT
STEALTH
SELF-CONTROL
STATUS-QUO
SURVEILLANCE
SITUATIONAL SENSE
STIMULI
SUSPICION
SKILL-SETS
SOCIETY
SUPPLIES
SYMBOLS
SELF-DISCIPLINE
STRIDE
SMELL
SECRECY
STEREOTYPES
STRUCTURES
SECURITY
SOUND
SCENARIOS
SAFETY
HIDDEN SUCCESS TACTICAL
www.hiddensuccesstactical.com
Copyright © 2020 Matthew Dermody. All rights reserved.

7 DEADLY SINS
THAT WILL DESTROY YOUR GRAY MAN ATTEMPTS
AMBIVALENCE
BOREDOM
COMPLACENCY of CONTEXT
DISTRACTIONS
ESCALATION of EGO
FAILING TO FIX FAILURES
GUESSING
HIDDEN SUCCESS TACTICAL
www.hiddensuccesstactical.com
Copyright © 2020 Matthew Dermody. All rights reserved.

HOW TO iNCREASE SITUATIONAL SENSE

1. Acknowledge risks and potential dangers.
2. Substantiate/verify risks against local law enforcement records or reports.
3. Define your personal space requirements.
4. Identify actions that trigger your suspicion or anxiety.
5. Create a mitigation/contingency plan.
6. Obtain/practice the skills necessary to execute your plan.
7. Adjust/modify physiological saboteurs (i.e. food, sleep, exercise, alcohol consumption).
8. Turn off all unnecessary electronic and technology distractions.
9. Avoid multi-tasking when possible.
10. Use the Pan-Tilt-Zoom method of aware observation.
11. Give yourself time and room to move.
12. Warn others.

www.hiddensuccesstactical.com

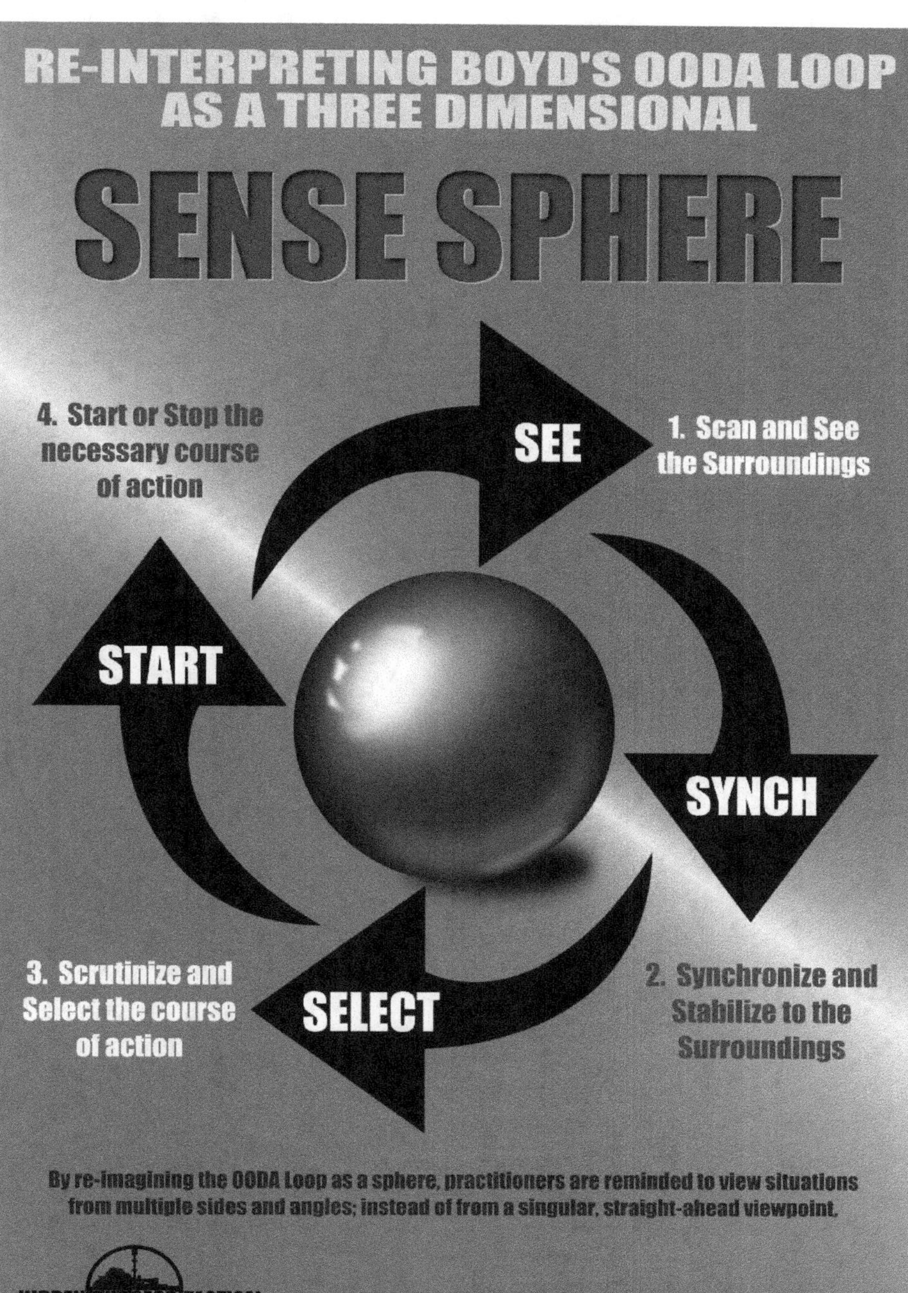
RE-INTERPRETING BOYD'S OODA LOOP AS A THREE DIMENSIONAL
SENSE SPHERE
4. Start or Stop the necessary course of action
SEE
1. Scan and See the Surroundings
START
SYNCH
3. Scrutinize and Select the course of action
SELECT
2. Synchronize and Stabilize to the Surroundings
By re-imagining the OODA Loop as a sphere, practitioners are reminded to view situations from multiple sides and angles; instead of from a singular, straight-ahead viewpoint.
HIDDEN SUCCESS TACTICAL
www.hiddensuccesstactical.com
Copyright © 2020 Matthew Dermody. All rights reserved.

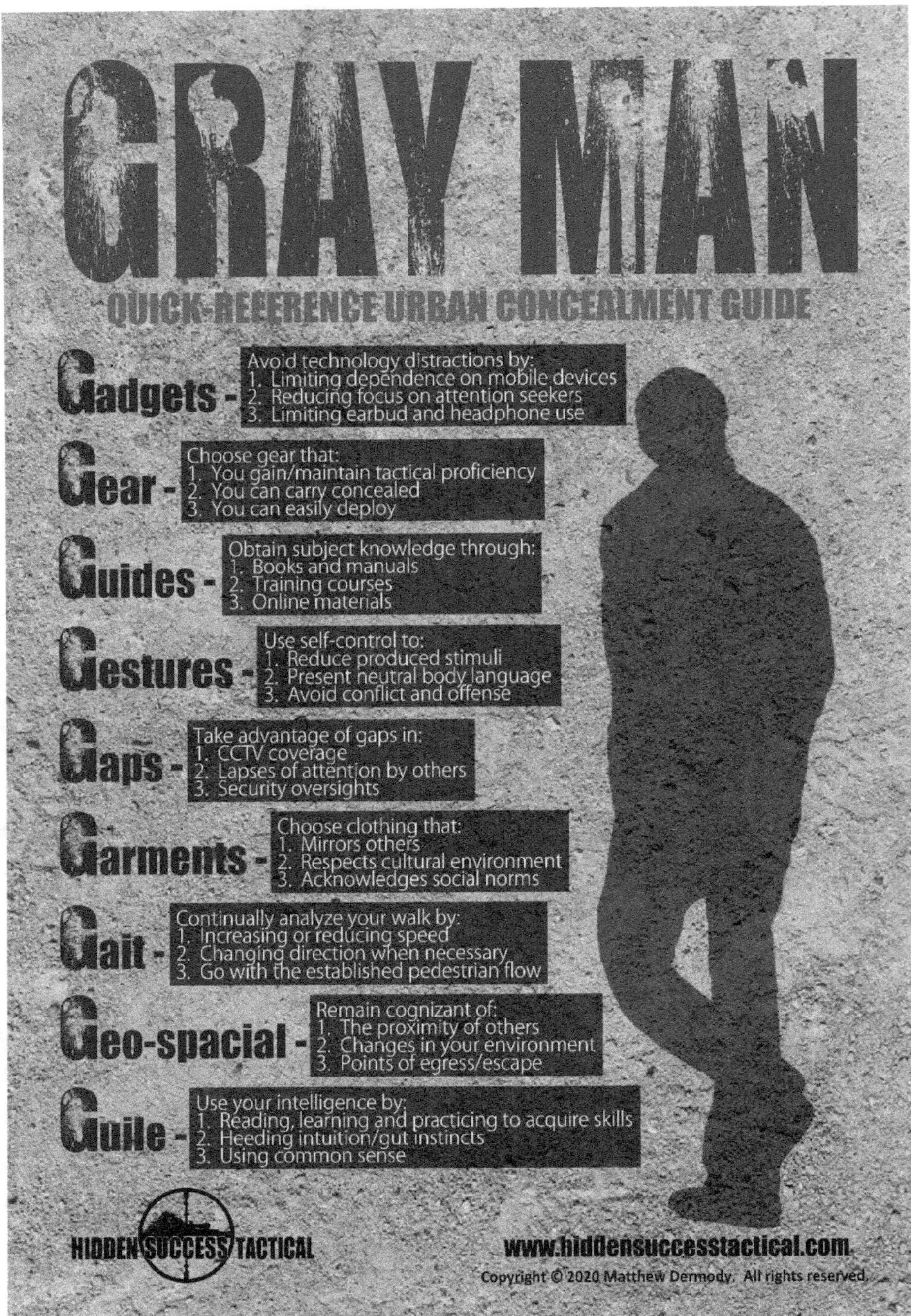
GRAY MAN
QUICK-REFERENCE URBAN CONCEALMENT GUIDE

Gadgets -
Avoid technology distractions by:
1. Limiting dependence on mobile devices
2. Reducing focus on attention seekers
3. Limiting earbud and headphone use

Gear -
Choose gear that:
1. You gain/maintain tactical proficiency
2. You can carry concealed
3. You can easily deploy

Guides -
Obtain subject knowledge through:
1. Books and manuals
2. Training courses
3. Online materials

Gestures -
Use self-control to:
1. Reduce produced stimuli
2. Present neutral body language
3. Avoid conflict and offense

Gaps -
Take advantage of gaps in:
1. CCTV coverage
2. Lapses of attention by others
3. Security oversights

Garments -
Choose clothing that:
1. Mirrors others
2. Respects cultural environment
3. Acknowledges social norms

Gait -
Continually analyze your walk by:
1. Increasing or reducing speed
2. Changing direction when necessary
3. Go with the established pedestrian flow

Geo-spacial -
Remain cognizant of:
1. The proximity of others
2. Changes in your environment
3. Points of egress/escape

Guile -
Use your intelligence by:
1. Reading, learning and practicing to acquire skills
2. Heeding intuition/gut instincts
3. Using common sense

HIDDEN SUCCESS TACTICAL
www.hiddensuccesstactical.com
Copyright © 2020 Matthew Dermody. All rights reserved.

SOVI3T SYLLABUS

AKA THE MOSCOW RULES

FOR GRAY MAN TACTICS AND SITUATIONAL AWARENESS

1. Assume nothing.
2. Never go against your gut.
3. Everyone is potentially under opposition control.
4. Do not look back; you are never completely alone.
5. Go with the flow, blend in.
6. Vary your pattern and stay within your cover.
7. Lull them into a sense of complacency.
8. Do not harass the opposition.
9. Pick the time and place for action.
10. Keep your options open.

Source: https://en.wikipedia.org/wiki/The_Moscow_rules

SITUATIONAL SENSE
VEHICLE PROCEDURES

ARRIVING AND PREPARING TO EXIT VEHICLE...

1. **STOP** — Stop the vehicle and shut off the engine....

2. **STOW** — Stow personal items and secure valuables.

3. **SCAN** — Scan for potential threats and familiarize yourself to the area.

4. **STEP** — Step out and lock the vehicle. Remember the parking location.

APPROACHING VEHICLE AND DEPARTING...

1.  **SPOT** — Spot your vehicle. Have your keys in hand.

2. **SCAN** — Scan for potential threats. Unlock vehicle.

3. **STOW** — Stow parcels and seat passengers.

4. **SECURE** — Secure doorlocks. Situate. Seatbelt. Start the engine.

www.hiddensuccesstactical.com

<u>Glossary of Acronyms</u>

BOB – An acronym for **B**ug **O**ut **B**ag. A backpack or rucksack consisting of supplies and survival items, with consumables (food, batteries, clothing, etc.) intended to last 72 hours or less before the need for replenishment.

COA – An acronym for **C**ourse **o**f **A**ction. An executable plan based upon decisions made factoring in the current available intelligence or known circumstances.

CCW – An acronym for **C**oncealed **C**arry **W**eapon. This is usually referenced in conjunction with a license or permit issued by a state government for the lawful, discreet carry of a weapon, usually a firearm.

CUE – An acronym for **C**ivil **U**nrest **E**vent. A major civil disturbance marked by violent protesting, rioting, looting, active mayhem, and resulting destruction of public and private property.

EDC – An acronym for **E**very-**D**ay **C**arry. Personal items and/or tools carried by an individual to assist in dealing and overcoming unforeseen events or predictable scenarios.

EDW – An acronym for **E**very-**D**ay **W**ear. Personal clothing choices made based upon weather, culture, comfort, and practicality.

EEE – An acronym for **E**ngage/**E**vade/**E**scape. This primarily addresses the "fight or flight" decision making process in a conflict.

GHB – An acronym for **G**et **H**ome **B**ag. A small backpack or daypack designed to carry supplies and survival items intended to last 24 hours or less to return to a current place of residence.

GOOD Bag – An acronym for **G**et **O**ut **o**f **D**odge. Similar in concept to the Bug Out Bag. By using the term "good" bag, if overheard, it might be ignored as a conversation about the quality of a bag, rather than its purpose.

HAMPERR – An acronym for **H**abits, **A**ppearance, **M**annerisms, **P**atronage, **E**ye contact, **R**epeat **R**ecognition.

ICE – An acronym for 1.) **I**n **C**ase of **E**mergency or 2.) **I**ncited **C**risis **E**vent.

IFAK – An acronym for **I**ndividual **F**irst **A**id **K**it. A basic medical supply kit used to treat minor, acute injuries, and exposures.

INCH Bag – An acronym for **I**'m **N**ever **C**oming **H**ome and is a last resort mindset shift from the BOB. Circumstances have permanently affected your ability or desire to stay at a governmental or environmental level, where staying domiciled would increase the likelihood of injury or death.

LEAVE – An emergency escape plan acronym for **L**ocate, **E**vade, **A**ccess/**A**ctivate, maintain **V**igilance, **E**xit. Primarily used when PACE planning or other scouting/reconnaissance efforts could not be done prior to insertion into an unfamiliar area.

NPE – An acronym for Non-Permissive Environment. Occupying/controlling forces within an area or region that impose extremely strict sanctions on area access, items in your possession, and restrict movement within that controlled environment.

OPSEC – A military abbreviation for **OP**erations **SEC**urity. The intentional withholding of specific, mission related movements and positions to prevent unauthorized disclosure to a known enemy or other unauthorized persons, including family and friends.

PACE – An acronym for the strategic planning method of creating four distinct plans: **P**rimary **A**lternate **C**ontingency **E**mergency.

POI – An acronym for **P**erson **of I**nterest. The person may be the subject of a surveillance mission or investigation. When implementing Gray Man principles, you do not want to become the targeted focus of someone else's attention or interest.

PERSEC – A military abbreviation for **PER**sonal **SEC**urity. Proactive and responsive measures/countermeasures taken to ensure individual safety.

SAFE – An acronym for **S**ubtleness **A**stuteness **F**inesse **E**fficiency, attributes needed for the implementation of Gray Man principles.

SERE – A military acronym for **S**urvival **E**vasion **R**esistance **E**scape. A deliberate attempt to avoid capture by an enemy force or attempt to escape from confinement, detention, or imprisonment while making every effort to thwart interrogation and questioning regarding sensitive and critical intelligence. (i.e., force numbers, supply chains, troop movements, etc.)

SHTF – An acronym for **S**hit **H**its **t**he **F**an. A catastrophic event usually signifying a manmade crisis that temporarily alters or interrupts the current status quo within an environment. It can also describe natural disaster events that interrupt infrastructure or relief efforts.

SOP – A military acronym for **S**tandard **O**perating **P**rocedure. A set of instructions providing step-by-step course(s) of action in accordance with governing policies and legislation.

TEOTWAWKI – An acronym for **T**he **E**nd **o**f **t**he **W**orld **a**s **W**e **K**now **I**t. Catastrophic events on a global scale which permanently disrupt all sense of normalcy, with great loss of life, and a subsequent domino effect collapsing essential services, utilities, currency, commodities, and supply chains.

TROUBLE Kit – An acronym for **T**errorism **R**iots **O**ccupations **U**nrest **B**lockades **L**awlessness **E**vasion/**E**ngage/**E**scape. A rapidly deployed backpack filled with tools to circumvent or deny access, pretextually assimilate into hostile environments for the purpose of escaping rapidly developing civil unrest events.

VEK – An acronym for **V**ehicle **E**mergency **K**it. A small bag containing supplies in the event an individual's vehicle becomes stranded or immobilized due to weather conditions, breakdown, or collision.

WET – An acronym for **W**arranted **E**xternal **T**hreats

WROL – An acronym for **W**ithout **R**ule **o**f **L**aw. Circumstances or events have occurred politically or environmentally where the active presence of law enforcement has been curtailed, removed, or otherwise rendered ineffective in its duty to maintain law and order.

6C – An abbreviated acronym (pronounced "Six Charlie") describing the incremental decline of civilization with an ascending scale from lower to greater severity. Each of the six stages starts with the letter "C" or Charlie in the phonetic alphabet. They are **C**risis, **C**atastrophe, **C**ollapse, **C**haos, **C**onflict, **C**alamity.

Training Resources, Affiliates & Products

Kamouflage LTD – https://www.kamouflage.co.uk/

Superesse Straps – https://www.superessestraps.com/

Gray Man Brief – https://www.instagram.com/graymanbrief/

Bug Out Vehicle – https://www.instagram.com/bugoutvehicle/

Off The Grid Guide – https://www.instagram.com/offthegridguide/

Gray.Man.Project – https://www.instagram.com/gray.man.project/

Gutter Fighting Secrets – https://www.gutterfightingsecrets.com/

Covert Products Group – https://www.covertproductsgroup.com/

True North Tradecraft – https://truenorthtradecraft.ca/

Old Gray Man Club – https://www.facebook.com/OldGrayManClub/

Black Scout Survival – https://blackscoutsurvival.com/

OnPoint Tactical – https://onpointtactical.com/

The Diamond Arrow Group – https://thediamondarrowgroup.com/

Sigma III Survival – https://survivalschool.us/

Spycraft 101 – https://spycraft101.com/

The Warrior's Path Academy – https://thewarriorspathacademy.com/

Arcadia Cognerati – https://www.instagram.com/arcadia_cognerati/

Gunsite Academy – https://www.gunsite.com/

IMTT USA – https://imtt.net/index.html

Scott-Donelan Tracking School – https://mantrack1.com/

Spearpoint Training Group – https://sptraininggroup.com/

Option Gray – https://optiongray.com/

Tracer Tactical – https://tracer-tactical.com/

Nature Reliance School – https://naturereliance.org/

Grey Man Tactical – https://greymantactical.com/

Additional Resources

- ACM IV Security Services, *Secrets of Surveillance: A Professional's Guide to Tailing Subjects by Vehicle, Foot, Airplane, and Public Transportation*, Paladin Press, September 1, 1993

- Ahearn, Frank & Horan, Eileen, *How to Disappear: Erase Your Digital Footprint, Leave Fake Trails, and Vanish Without a Trace*, Lyons Press, 2010

- Alwood, Kelly, *Behavioral Programming: The Manipulation of Social Interaction*, CreateSpace Independent Publishing Platform, May 25, 2015

- Black Scout Survival, *How to Become the "Gray Man" - Urban Survival*, YouTube video, 2013

- Black Scout Survival, *Escape and Evasion: Covert Concealment/ Grayman Tradecraft*, YouTube video, 2015

- "Becoming the Gray Man" - www.truprepper.com/article/becoming-gray-man-skill-constant-camouflage/, May 14, 2016

- Cooper, Jeff, *Mental Conditioning*, Gunsite/American Pistol Institute video

- Department of the Army, *Guerilla Warfare Handbook*, Skyhorse, January 27, 2009

- Dermody, Matthew, *Appear to Vanish: Stealth Concepts for Effective Camouflage and Concealment*, Paladin Press, May 2017

- Dermody, Matthew, *Gray Man: Camouflage for Crowds, Cities, and Civil Crisis*, CreateSpace Independent Publishing Platform, September 2017

- Dermody, Matthew, *Conversational Camouflage: Oratory Discretion and Pretexting for Behavioral Concealment*, CreateSpace Independent Publishing Platform, October 2018

- Dermody, Matthew, *Situational Sense: Basic Threat Detection Using Situational Awareness and Common Sense*, independently published, December 2019

- Emerson, Clint with Walters, Lynn, *Escape the Wolf: Preemptive Personal Security Handbook* e-book, Escape the Wolf, September 9, 2012

- Jenkins, Peter, *Surveillance Tradecraft: The Professional's Guide to Covert Surveillance Training*, Intel Publications, March 30, 2010

- Kolkman, Russ, "How to 'Blend In' in an urban survival scenario", YouTube video, May 28, 2013

- Lotto, Beau, "Optical Illusions Show Us How We See," https://www.ted.com/talks/beau_lotto_optical_illusions_show_how_we_see

- Luna, J.J., *How to Be Invisible: Protect Your Home, Your Children, Your Assets, and Your Life*, Thomas Dune Books, 3rd Edition, 2012

- Mack, Jefferson, *Invisible Resistance to Tyranny*, Paladin Press, 2002

- MacInaugh, Edmund A., *Disguise Techniques: Fool All of the People Some of the Time*, Paladin Press, 1984

- Mendez, Antonio & Jonna w/Baglio, Matt, *The Moscow Rules: The Secret CIA Tactics That Helped America Win the Cold War*, Public Affairs reprint, May 19, 2020

- Ritch, Van, *Do You See What I'm Saying? - Secrets of Body Language Made Simple*, Paladin Press DVD

- Robideau, Rob, *Incognito Toolkit: Tools, Apps, and Creative Methods for Remaining Anonymous, Private, and Secure While Communicating, Publishing, Buying, and Researching Online*, Personal Armament, 2014

- Sample, John, *Methods of Disguise*, Loompanics Unlimited, 2nd edition, 1993

- Starnater, Eddie, *Principles of Natural Camouflage: The Science of Invisibility*, CreateSpace Independent Publishing Platform, November 6, 2015

- https://en.wikipedia.org/wiki/Decision-making

- Vickers, Joan A., *Perception, Cognition, and Decision Training - The Quiet Eye in Action*, Human Kinetics, June 10, 2007

- Waldron, Lee, http://www.realworldsurvivor.com/2015/09/24/becoming-the-gray-man-10-ways-blend-in-and-survive/#gray-man-7

- http://www.itstactical.com/intellicom/mindset/gray-man-strategies-101-peeling-away-the-thin-veneer-of-society/

- http://www.innovateus.net/health/what-function-reticular-activating-system

- http://www.meaningfulhq.com/reticular-activating-system-function.html

- https://forwardobserver.com/building-blocks-of-intelligence-salute-and-salt-reporting/

- http://mastermindmatrix.com/knowledge-base/reticular-activating-system/

- http://www.itstactical.com/intellicom/diy/deceive-a-mugger-with-a-diy-decoy-wallet/

About the Author

Matthew Dermody is a writer of eight previously self-published books as well as the occasional guest blogs and articles on subjects of camouflage and concealment, situational awareness, and personal security. He lives in Australia with his wife and twin daughters.

He has recently launched his own line of camouflage patterns under the branding of SUBSTRATE Baseline Camouflage. You may visit www.substrate-camo.com for more information regarding patterns and availability.